D1370219

POWER DRINKS

& ENERGY TONICS

POWER DRINKS
& ENERGY TONICS

TRACY RUTHERFORD

PERIPLUS

Contents

WITHDRAWN
WISSER MEMORIAL LIBRARY
WITHDRAWN
WITHDRAWN
TX815
.R87
2002
Copy

Juice Plans 101

Three-day cleansing juice plan
- • Day one
- • Day two
- • Day three
- • Pre-exam juice plan
- • Tips for studying
- • Sporting-event juice plan
- • The big event juice plan

Glossary 107

Index 108

Guide to Weights and Measures 111

Recipes

Introduction

Power *Drinks and Energy Tonics* is a collection of juices, smoothies, shakes, and teas designed to provide maximum nutrition with a minimum of fuss. It is sometimes difficult to incorporate the recommended daily servings of fruit and vegetables into our diet, but juicing and blending offer convenient and delicious ways of doing so. These are also great ways to get children to consume more fruit, though juices should be diluted with purified water for young children, and the eating of whole fruits and vegetables encouraged as much as possible. If you have any kind of blood sugar disorder, it is also recommended that you dilute juices, as they do contain a concentrated supply of fruit sugars.

When making juices, the final product will only be as good as the ingredients used, so always choose fruits and vegetables that are ripe, but not overly so, and that look bright and fresh. Use produce in season, as it will be cheaper, fresher, and in optimum condition. If you can, buy organic produce, as many fruits and vegetables are juiced with their skin still on, and the skin may harbor residual chemicals. Also, if you are taking the time to create fresh juices at home, it makes sense to use the healthiest ingredients possible.

Unpeeled fruits and vegetables must always be cleaned thoroughly before use. Use a small, firm-bristled brush kept specifically for this purpose. If the produce is not organic, use a mild biodegradable detergent to remove all traces of chemicals, and rinse thoroughly. The recipes indicate how each fruit or vegetable is to be prepared for juicing, usually they just need to be chopped into pieces that will fit into the feed tube. You may want to chill produce before juicing for some recipes, but this is a matter of taste.

Juicers vary considerably in power and efficiency. If you have an older or slightly less-efficient juicer, you may find you need to add small pieces like berries and grapes to the feed tube while the motor is turned off, then turn it on and plunge them all together. Fresh herbs and other leaves should be placed between fleshier pieces of fruit or vegetable where possible, to help extract as much juice as possible. We have given approximate yields for each drink, though this will vary depending on your equipment and produce.

The combinations of ingredients given for the drinks may be varied to suit your taste and their availability. Some of the recipes list optional ingredients. These are mostly supplements with specific applications that may be useful to athletes or to treat ailments. Feel free to use them or not, or to seek further information about them from a naturopath or your natural food store.

The drinks in this book provide concentrated nutrition, and some can be used to assist in the treatment of specific conditions, but you should always consult a health-care professional for advice. Most of the drinks are delicious, as you would expect from the combinations of fresh, juicy fruits and vegetables, while some are slightly more medicinal. Each chapter is devoted to a specific use, though fruits, vegetables, and other ingredients that may help one condition usually are good for others as well.

Equipment

The pieces of equipment required to make the drinks in this book are a blender, a juicer, a grinder, and a citrus juicer. You probably already have some of these, but if you are shopping for new appliances consider the following factors and choose the best quality you can afford.

Juicer

- ♨ Check for ease of cleaning and assembling. Does the juicer have a lot of components to deal with, or does it have grooves or other hard-to-clean crevices? Look for a simple, streamlined machine.
- ♨ What is the size and position of pulp container? If making large quantities of juice, will you have to stop and take the machine apart often to clear out pulp, and if so, is it easy to do? Some juicers have external pulp collection areas, which means you don't have to disassemble anything to empty them.
- ♨ How powerful is the motor? Will it extract the maximum amount of juice?
- ♨ Check for safety and ease of use. Does the lid have a safety lock? Are the controls easy to use?

Similar considerations apply to blenders, electric citrus juicers, and grinders. If you are still unsure, look at the brand reputation and the warranty conditions in case something does go wrong. It is also a good idea to check consumer guides for price and workability comparisons.

Another important point to consider is where you will keep your machine. Do you have room on your countertop to leave it set up all the time? Will it fit in an easy-to-reach cupboard? Accessibility is vital, as many juicers are bought with the best intentions, only to languish, forgotten, in dark cupboards.

Blender

Grinder

Juice extractor: Centrifugal

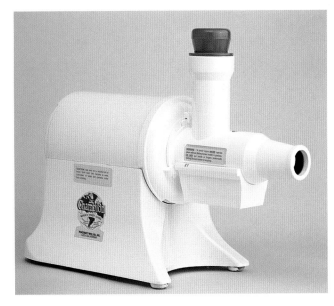

Juice extractor: Masticating

Citrus juicer: Reamer

Citrus juicer: Manual juicer

Citrus juicer: Electric juicer

Citrus juicer: Press/lever juicer

Blender

A blender is used to liquidize soft fruits for drinks, as well as to make milk-based shakes and smoothies. Be sure yours will handle ice cubes, which can overwork less powerful motors. If not, wrap ice cubes in a clean tea towel and crush them with a rolling pin or mallet before blending.

Grinder

A grinder is used to grind nuts and seeds to a meal or fine powder. This not only changes them into a form suitable for drinks, but also in some cases makes them more digestible. An electric coffee grinder is probably the most efficient grinder, but you will need to keep it specifically for nuts and seeds, so as not to transfer a coffee flavor.

Juice Extractors

There are different types of extractors, but the two types normally used in domestic situations are either a centrifugal extractor or a masticating extractor, with the former being the most common.

A centrifugal machine extracts juice by finely grating food, then using centrifugal force (spinning around very fast) to separate the juice from the pulp. This tends to aerate the juice, which should be consumed straight away, as it will deteriorate rapidly.

A masticating machine also finely grates the food, but then has a "chewing" action that makes the particles even smaller. This pulp is pressed to extract the juice, so it doesn't incorporate air. This means that the juice can be stored for up to one day in the refrigerator.

Citrus Juicers

Citrus fruits can be peeled and juiced in an extractor, but if you are only juicing one or two pieces of a citrus fruit, you may want to use a citrus juicer. There are four kinds:

Reamer: A small handheld tool with a handle at one end and a corrugated, rounded cone at the other. The reamer is inserted into the cut fruit and twisted to extract juice.

Manual juicer: A small, freestanding juicer with a "cone" standing upright, with either a juice collection gutter around it or holes draining into a jug. The cut fruit is twisted by hand to extract the juice.

Electric juicer: A comparatively large piece of equipment, the cut fruit is held in place by hand, while a motor spins the "cone." The juice drains through a spout into a collection pitcher.

Press/lever juicer: This type of manual juicer has styles that can vary slightly, but they work on the principle of the pressure—the cut citrus half is placed on the cone, then you pull a lever to exert pressure, releasing the juice. These are very stylish pieces, usually made from stainless steel with some chrome parts.

Ingredients and Supplements

Dairy and Non-dairy Products

Acidophilus yogurt is made with the bacteria culture *Lactobacillus acidophilus*. Eating this yogurt helps restore the intestinal bacteria lost through illness or the use of antibiotics.

Coconut milk is made by squeezing liquid from grated coconut flesh. It is available in cans in most supermarkets.

Cows' milk is the most widely used kind of milk, and thus one of the most common sources of calcium. Some people, however, have an intolerance to lactose, the sugar present in milk, and must use an alternative.

Oat milk is an alternative to cows' milk, made from whole-grain oats, a little oil, and water. Found in cartons in natural food stores and some supermarkets.

Rice milk, another milk alternative, is made from whole-grain brown rice and usually contains some kind of oil, a little salt, and water. Available in cartons from natural food stores and some supermarkets.

Soy milk is made from soybeans and may contain other ingredients such as malt, oil, and rice syrup. Choose calcium-fortified brands, and look for organic soy milk whenever possible to avoid a genetically modified product, as well as undesirable chemicals.

Soy yogurt is made from soy milk. Look for brands that contain acidophilus culture.

Silken tofu is another soy product, made by adding a setting agent to soy milk. Tofu can either be firm or soft, the latter is best for drinks and desserts, as it has a very soft texture.

Liquids

Barley water is made by boiling pearl barley in water and draining off the resulting liquid, which is slightly thick. It is very nutritious.

Coconut water is the clear liquid found in the center of a coconut. It is obtained by piercing the coconut shell with a sharp implement, such as a pick, tapped with a hammer.

Rose water is a flavoring used in Middle Eastern and Indian cooking. It is also said to have cooling, nourishing properties. Available from natural foods stores or specialty markets.

Acidophilus yogurt

Coconut milk

Cows' milk

Oat milk

Rice milk

Soy milk

Soy yogurt

Silken tofu

Barley water

Coconut water

Rose water

Herbal Preparations and Nutritional Supplements

Aloe vera juice is squeezed from the succulent leaves of the aloe vera plant. It is claimed to have many healing properties, and is available in bottles in the refrigerator at natural foods stores.

Blackstrap molasses is a by-product of sugar refining, and is the lowest grade of molasses, with dark color and slightly bitter flavor. It is rich in calcium and iron, among other nutrients. It is available from natural foods stores.

Brewer's yeast is a good natural source of B vitamins, protein, and chromium. It comes in a powder form, from natural foods stores. Do not confuse it with other types of yeast.

Chlorophyll liquid is a concentrated form of the substance that gives the green color to plants. It has healing properties and is often used to treat bad breath and body odor. Available from natural foods stores.

Echinacea drops are the liquid form of the immune-boosting herb echinacea. It is thought to be particularly useful at the onset of a cold or other respiratory ailments. Available from natural foods stores or herbal-medicine practitioners.

Ginkgo drops are the liquid form of the herb ginkgo biloba. It is said to stimulate circulation, relieve tinnitus, and aid memory. Available from natural foods stores.

Glucosamine is a substance that the body needs to build and repair cartilage and to maintain healthy joints. As a supplement, it may be useful to athletes or osteoarthritis sufferers. It comes in powder form from natural foods stores.

Guarana powder is made from ground seed of Paullinia cupana, a Brazilian rain-forest tree. It contains some caffeine and therefore has an "energy boost" effect similar to coffee. Available from natural foods stores and some supermarkets.

L-carnitine is an amino acid that helps the body to metabolize fat and utilize it as fuel. It comes in powder form from natural foods stores.

Aloe vera juice

Blackstrap molasses

Brewer's yeast

Chlorophyll liquid

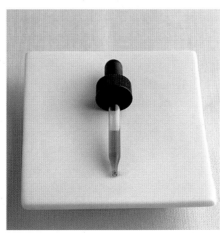

Echinacea drops

Ginkgo drops

Glucosamine

Guarana powder

L-carnitine

Lecithin is a substance that assists in the breakdown of fats and cholesterol. It may help to combat fat-related conditions such as arterial disease and gallstones. Available in granule form from natural foods stores.

Slippery elm powder is a finely ground bark. It is used mainly to soothe inflamed mucous membranes anywhere in the digestive system. Available from natural foods stores.

Protein whey powder is a dairy by-product. It is a source of amino acids, which are needed for muscle tissue maintenance. You can buy it as an expensive sports drink powder, which includes other ingredients (such as sugar and flavorings), or as a less expensive, unadorned supplement from health foods stores.

Spirulina powder is made from various types of algae, and has a concentration of many nutrients. It is believed to be a good source of protein, especially for vegetarians, as it contains all the essential amino acids. Available from natural foods stores.

Psyllium husks are a gentle soluble fiber that passes through the body, helping to remove waste. Available from natural foods stores and some supermarkets.

Wheat germ is part of the wheat grain, discarded in the processing of white flour. It is very nutritious, rich in vitamin E and B vitamins. Available from natural foods stores and supermarkets.

Wheatgrass is a grass grown from wheat grain and harvested at a particular stage to yield the optimum concentration of nutrients. It is reputed to be an excellent source of vitamins (particularly B, C and E) and minerals (calcium, magnesium, potassium, and iron), as well as enzymes, amino acids, and chlorophyll. It must be made into juice to be properly digested.

Wheatgrass juice is the liquified form of wheatgrass. Regular domestic centrifugal juicers are not capable of producing wheatgrass juice, so either seek out a model which is, or purchase from the refrigerator section at health foods stores. It is highly perishable, and must be used within 36 hours of production.

Lecithin

Slippery elm powder

Protein whey powder

Spirulina powder

Psyllium husks

Wheat germ

Wheatgrass

Wheatgrass juice

Creating Flavor

Sweeteners

Palm sugar, used in Southeast Asian cooking, is made from the sap of coconut and palmyrah palms. The color varies from dark brown to light golden, and it has a crumbly texture. It is available in block form from specialty foods markets and natural foods stores.

Honey is widely available but varies in quality and flavor. Use raw honey (honey that has not been heated) from a natural foods store if possible.

Carob powder, ground from roasted carob pods, is similar in appearance, flavor, and texture to cocoa powder. Though not strictly a sweetener, it is often used as a chocolate substitute. It has many vitamins and minerals, and no caffeine.

Nuts and Seeds

Almond meal is simply almonds ground to a fine powder. You can buy it or make it yourself using a grinder.

Brazil nuts, sometimes known as para nuts, are a good source of magnesium. These relatively large, elongated, three-sided nuts originated in Brazil.

Flaxseed (linseed) meal is finely ground flaxseed. It is best to grind your own, as the oils tend to deteriorate quickly once ground.

Flaxseed oil is available in bottles from refrigerators in natural foods stores. It is highly perishable, so keep refrigerated and use before the marked expiry date.

Peanut butter is a paste made from ground peanuts. Choose natural peanut butter from natural foods stores, rather than varieties with added salt and sugar.

Sunflower seed meal must be made by grinding sunflower seeds, as it is not available already ground. The seeds are a good source of thiamine, vitamin E, and silicon.

Tahini is a paste made from sesame seeds. Commonly used in Middle Eastern dishes such as hummus, it is rich in minerals, particularly calcium, phosphorus, and magnesium.

NUTS AND SEEDS
Top: Flaxseed oil
Second row (left to right): Tahini, Peanut butter
Third row (left to right): Flaxseed meal, Brazil nuts
Bottom row (left to right): Sunflower seed meal, Almond meal

Spices

Asafoetida is a ground spice derived from a plant grown in India and the Middle East. In herbal medicine it is used to ease coughs and other respiratory problems, and to reduce gas. Also known as hing.

Black pepper is ground from dried black peppercorns. It is best to buy whole peppercorns and grind them yourself. Pepper aids digestion and circulation.

Cardamom, commonly used in Indian cooking, is available as whole pods, seeds, or ground. Cardamom is good for digestion, coughs, and colds.

Cinnamon can be bought ground or in stick form, as a piece of rolled bark. Used in both sweet and savory dishes, cinnamon is good for circulation and digestion.

Coriander seeds come from the cilantro, or fresh coriander, plant, and are used whole or ground. Found in many countries, coriander is an important component of various spice blends. It stimulates the digestive system and helps with urinary tract infections.

Cayenne pepper is ground from the dried cayenne chili. Used to add heat and spice in cooking, it also enhances circulation, is good for digestion, and acts as a decongestant.

Fenugreek seeds come from a plant that is a member of the pea family. Usually ground and added to curry blends, fenugreek has anti-inflammatory properties and is an expectorant.

Ginger is used fresh or dried and ground. It is good for digestion, circulation, and nausea, and is used in many sweet and savory dishes.

Saffron threads are the dried stigmas from a kind of crocus. It is hand-harvested and therefore quite expensive. Used in cooking for its flavor and to add a golden color to foods; in herbal medicine it is used to treat depression.

Vanilla extract is made from the vanilla bean, a highly fragrant pod containing tiny black seeds. It is used to flavor many sweet dishes and baked goods.

Nutmeg is a ground spice commonly used in sweet milky or egg-based desserts. Medicinally, it is used to help induce sleep.

SPICES
Top: Vanilla extract
Second row (left to right): Ground fenugreek, Ground coriander, Ground cardamom, Cinnamon sticks
Third row (left to right): Cayenne pepper, Ground ginger, Ground cinnamon, Ground black pepper
Bottom row (left to right): Coriander seeds, Ground nutmeg, Asafoetida, Saffron threads

Cleansing

We spend a lot of time and energy cleaning our homes, clothes, hair, and skin, but often neglect to cleanse the inside of our bodies. Toxins and wastes aren't always efficiently cleared out of the system, mainly because we live in an environment of overload.

Our foods are processed and contain artificial colors, flavors and preservatives. Alcohol is consumed daily, and tap water is the source of many undesirable elements. The air we breathe and the products we use all contribute to a buildup of toxins. At best, this makes us feel lethargic and slightly unwell; at worst it can lead to serious illness.

What to do? Cleansing and detoxifying regimes can vary in intensity from a fasting program to subtle changes in diet and lifestyle. Any major diet restrictions should be closely supervised by a naturopath or physician, and complete fasts are not recommended, especially without professional advice. Several factors are important if you want to cleanse your system. First, cut out all processed foods and base your diet on foods as close to their natural state as possible. Eat lots of raw salads, dressed simply with a squeeze of lemon juice. Cooked vegetables should be lightly steamed, or stir-fried in a tiny amount of cold-pressed oil. Coffee, alcohol, and soft drinks should be eliminated from the diet. See pages 100–103 for a simple three-day cleansing program.

Secondly, make sure the organs of the body that regulate cleansing and elimination are working properly. The liver plays an important role in removing toxins from the system, and a healthy, low-fat diet is needed to maintain optimum function. The consumption of alcohol, saturated fats, spicy foods, tea, and coffee all increase the workload of the liver and should be kept to a minimum. The kidneys also assist in elimination by filtering out toxins. Many drinks in this chapter have ingredients that stimulate the liver and kidneys, and that are naturally laxative and diuretic.

It is also important to examine your immediate environment for anything that could be harmful. Avoid excessive use of chemical-based cleaning products, so-called "air fresheners," and pesticides. Recent research suggests we are overcleaning our homes, thanks to scare tactics by companies advertising their cleaning products. Some cleaning products are more harmful than a little grime!

Super "Orange" Juice

This is a good juice for days when you are eating lightly, perhaps after a time of over-indulgence. Mango soothes the mucous membranes of the stomach and intestine, and is considered in Ayurvedic medicine to have rejuvenative properties; while papaya contains the enzyme papain, which aids digestion. Pineapple has appetite-supressing enzymes. Both mango and papaya are high in beta-carotene, an antioxidant that helps to eliminate free radicals from the body. They also have significant amounts of the powerful antioxidant vitamin C, as do orange and pineapple.

1 orange, peeled, seeded, and chopped
1/2 mango, peeled and cut from pit
1/2 small papaya, peeled, seeded, and chopped
1/4 pineapple, peeled, cored, and chopped

In a juicer, process all the ingredients.
Makes about 2 cups (16 fl oz/500 ml); serves 2

Prune and Apple Drink

Prunes are a natural laxative, and apples provide soluble fiber in the form of pectin. Psyllium husks help eliminate toxins, and black currants are high in antioxidants.

4 pitted prunes
3/4 cup (6 fl oz/180 ml) water
2 apples, unpeeled, cored, and chopped
1 cup (4 oz/125 g) fresh, or thawed frozen, black currants or blueberries
2 teaspoons psyllium husks

In a small saucepan, combine the prunes and water and bring to a boil. Reduce heat, cover, and simmer, for 10 minutes. Let cool. In a juicer, process the apples and black currants. In a blender, combine the apple-currant juice and the prunes and their liquid. Blend until smooth. Whisk in the psyllium husks and serve immediately.
Makes about 1 cup (8 fl oz/250 ml); serves 1

Grape and Dandelion Juice

Dandelions, generally thought of as a weed, are a valuable liver and blood cleanser. There are usually some lurking in the garden, but make sure that you identify them correctly and that they haven't been sprayed with an herbicide. Substitute 1/2 cup (1/2 oz/15 g) packed parsley sprigs if you have no access to dandelion leaves. The lecithin helps to break down and eliminate cholesterol, and the grapes are slightly laxative and cooling to the body.

2 cups (8 oz/250 g) red grapes
10 fresh dandelion leaves
1/2 lime, peeled, seeded, and chopped
1 teaspoon lecithin

In a juicer, alternately process folded dandelion leaves with grapes and pieces of lime to help the leaves through the blades. Stir in the lecithin (note that it will not completely dissolve).
Makes about 3/4 cup (6 fl oz/180 ml); serves 1

Right: Super "Orange" Juice

Orange, Ginger and Herb Drink

Basil is antibacterial and a blood purifier, and thyme is also antibacterial, particularly for the gastro-intestinal tract. Ginger stimulates circulation, and orange provides the antioxidant vitamin C.

4 fresh basil leaves, chopped
2 large sprigs thyme
1/2-inch (12-mm) piece fresh ginger, sliced
1 cup (8 fl oz/250 ml) boiling water
1 teaspoon honey
juice of 1 large orange

In a cup, combine the herbs and ginger. Add the boiling water. Let steep for 10 minutes, then strain. Stir in the honey, then the orange juice. Serve warm.
Makes about 1 1/4 cups (10 fl oz/300 ml); serves 1

Cranberry and Barley Drink

The cranberries in this drink are high in vitamin C and potassium, and are slightly diuretic, as well as having antiviral and antibacterial properties. The barley water is soothing and alkalizing, and helps to reduce cholesterol. You can purchase ready-made barley water, or make your own by combining 1/4 cup (2 oz/60 g) pearl barley and 3 cups (24 fl oz/750 ml) water in a saucepan. Bring to a boil then reduce heat and simmer until the liquid has reduced to 1/2 cup (4 fl oz/125 ml), about 30 minutes. Strain and let cool.

1 apple, unpeeled, cored, and chopped
1 1/4 cups (5 oz/150 g) fresh, or thawed frozen, cranberries
1/2 cup (4 oz/125 ml) barley water

In a juicer, process the apple and cranberries. Stir in the barley water.
Makes about 1 1/2 cups (12 fl oz/375 ml); serves 1

Spinach and Red Pepper Juice

This drink is high in antioxidants, which slow cellular-aging and degeneration, and it also contains calcium, folic acid, and iron. The cinnamon stimulates circulation and improves digestion.

2 cups (2 oz/60 g) packed fresh spinach leaves
1 large red bell pepper (capsicum), seeded and chopped
1 carrot, chopped
1/2-inch (12-mm) piece fresh ginger
large pinch ground cinnamon

In a juicer, process the spinach, bell pepper, carrot, and ginger. Whisk in the cinnamon.
Makes about 3/4 cup (6 fl oz/180 ml); serves 1

Left: Orange, Ginger and Herb Drink

Fennel, Pear and Mint Juice

This delicious drink helps with cleansing and elimination after a period of indulgence. The pear is mildly laxative, while the mint and asafoetida help to reduce gas and sweeten the breath.

1/2 fennel bulb, trimmed, and cored
2 pears, unpeeled, cored, and chopped
pinch asafoetida
10 fresh mint leaves, finely chopped

In a juicer, process the fennel and pears. Whisk in the asafoetida and mint.
Makes about 1 1/4 cups (10 fl oz/300 ml); serves 1

Mango and Lychee Juice

This is a very soothing, cooling drink. The mango soothes the mucous membranes of the stomach and intestine, while the lychees, coconut water, and rose water purify the blood. The coconut water is also diuretic, and good for the kidneys and urinary tract.

2 mangos, peeled and cut from pit
10 lychees, peeled and pitted
1 cup (8 fl oz/250 ml) coconut water
few drops rose water to taste (optional)

In a juicer, process the mango and lychees. Stir in the coconut water and the rose water, if desired. Serve immediately.
Makes about 2 cups (16 fl oz/500 ml); serves 2

Carrot, Celery and Arugula Juice

Celery works to purify the blood, kidneys, and bladder, and contains compounds that counter the effect of environmental pollutants. Fenugreek helps to lower blood pressure, purify the blood, and reduce gas.

1 fenugreek tea bag
1/2 cup (4 fl oz/125 ml) boiling water
1 carrot, chopped
1 1/2 cups (1 1/2 oz/45 g) packed fresh arugula leaves
2 stalks celery, chopped

Put the fenugreek tea bag in a cup and add the boiling water. Let steep for 10 minutes, then remove the tea bag and refrigerate the tea until cold, about 20 minutes. In a juicer, first process the carrot, then the arugula and celery. Pour in the tea and stir to combine.
Makes about 1 cup (8 fl oz/250 ml); serves 1

Right: Fennel, Pear and Mint Juice

INSTITUT
OGYLIBRAR

NEW YORK INSTITUTE
OF TECHNOLOGY LIBRARY

Cantaloupe, Blueberry and Mint Juice

Cantaloupe (rockmelon) contains the antioxidant beta-carotene, and its high water content helps to flush out the system. Blueberries contribute vitamin C, as well as antibacterial compounds, which help to combat gastro-intestinal and urinary tract infections. Mint is a digestive herb, and parsley is an effective diuretic.

1/2 cup (1/2 oz/15 g) packed parsley sprigs with stems
10 fresh mint leaves
1/2 cantaloupe (rockmelon), peeled, seeded, and chopped
1 cup (4 oz/125 g) fresh, or thawed frozen, blueberries

In a juicer, alternately process the parsley and mint with pieces of cantaloupe, then the blueberries. Stir to combine.
Makes about 1 1/2 cups (12 fl oz/375 ml); serves 1–2

Carrot, Apple and Cucumber Juice

This juice is very refreshing, as cucumber has a cooling effect on the body as well as being mildly diuretic. Apples are a good source of vitamin C and soluble fiber. The natural sugars in the apple provide energy, which is useful during a cleansing juice fast or semi-fast. Carrots are bursting with beta-carotene, a super antioxidant.

1 small cucumber, chopped
1 large apple, unpeeled, cored, and chopped
1 carrot, chopped

In a juicer, process all the ingredients.
Makes about 1 cup (8 fl oz/250 ml); serves 1

Watercress and Orange Juice

This drink has plenty of chlorophyll, a blood purifier. The lettuce has a high water content, which is cooling and cleansing, and the alfalfa aids digestion and lowers cholesterol. The vitamin C in the oranges helps the body utilize the iron in the watercress.

2 cups (2 oz/60 g) packed watercress sprigs
2 oz (60 g) alfalfa sprouts
2 large iceberg lettuce leaves
2 oranges, peeled, seeded, and chopped

In a juicer, process all the ingredients.
Makes about 1 cup (8 fl oz/250 ml); serves 1

Right: Cantaloupe, Blueberry and Mint Juice

Beet, Spinach and Pear Juice

Beets (beetroot) are a liver stimulant and a blood improver, and they help to cleanse the digestive system, as well as being rich in vitamins and minerals. Spinach contains carotenoids and vitamin C, both antioxidants that help to eliminate free radicals from the body. The pear adds soluble fiber and a sweet taste.

2 cups (2 oz/60 g) packed fresh spinach leaves
1 beet (beetroot), trimmed, unpeeled, and chopped
1 pear, unpeeled, cored, and chopped
filtered or spring water to taste (optional)

In a juicer, process the spinach, then the beet and pear. Dilute with a small amount of water to taste, if desired.
Makes about 3/4 cup (6 fl oz/180 ml); serves 1

Radish, Parsley and Carrot Juice

This peppery drink has diuretic properties. The radishes contain cancer-preventing compounds, as well as magnesium for muscle and nervous system function. The antioxidants in the carrots help to eliminate damaging free radicals.

2 radishes, trimmed and chopped
1 cup (1 oz/30 g) packed parsley sprigs with stems
2 large carrots, chopped

In a juicer, process the radishes, then the parsley and carrots.
Makes about 1 cup (8 fl oz/250 ml); serves 1

Peach, Plum and Raspberry Juice

Red-fleshed plums are one of the best fruit sources of antioxidants. Peaches contain potassium, which helps to eliminate waste and cleanse the system. Raspberries are said to cleanse and detoxify the digestive system, as well as being a good source of vitamin C, folate, and fiber. Psyllium husks aid elimination.

1 peach, unpeeled, pitted, and chopped
2 red-fleshed plums, pitted and chopped
1 cup (4 oz/125 g) fresh, or thawed frozen, raspberries
2 teaspoons psyllium husks

In a juicer, process all the fruit. Whisk in the psyllium husks and serve immediately.
Makes about 1 1/2 cups (12 fl oz/375 ml); serves 1

Left: Beet, Spinach and Pear Juice

Energy

Nutritionally, the word energy refers to the amount of calories (kilojoules) in a food. That doesn't mean this chapter is full of high-calorie drinks, however the drinks in this chapter offer energy in the form of fructose, or natural fruit sugars, combined with lots of vitamins and minerals to keep the body nourished. Whether you are employed in hard physical labor, sitting in an office, or running a house and meeting the demands of a family, you need to feel at your best at all times and to be able to cope with any crisis that may occur.

It is all too easy to reach for a candy bar, soft drink, or caffeine hit when you need a lift. The trouble with this is that even though you will have a fairly immediate rush of energy, it will not be sustained and you will end up feeling lower than you did in the first place. This often leads to another coffee or candy bar, creating a vicious circle of highs and lows.

Healthy drinks may be thought of as being time-consuming or difficult to make. Admittedly, if you are home during the day it is easier to make your own drinks, but if you are committed to a healthier lifestyle, it is not unreasonable to think about installing a juicer or blender in the office kitchen. Your coworkers will probably be interested in using it, helping to offset costs (or you could convince management of the increased productivity it will create!). Once you are in the habit of making juices or blended drinks every day, it will become second nature and not much more of a chore than making coffee.

For sustained energy levels throughout the day, make sure you start with a good breakfast, choosing natural cereals and whole grains, and avoiding commercial sugar-laden "breakfast foods." Have a nutritious lunch that includes protein and carbohydrates—a simple chicken or tunafish sandwich and salad is good—and a not too heavy evening meal. Between meals, snack on fresh and dried fruits, nuts, and drinks from this chapter.

Try to get some exercise during the day, especially if you work at a desk or any other sedentary occupation. Even just a walk around the block at lunchtime will re-energize you for the afternoon. It **is** amazing how expending energy can make you feel more energetic.

Banana and Mango Frappé

This drink is light and refreshing on a hot summer day, yet the banana makes it filling enough to provide energy between meals.

1 ripe banana, peeled and chopped
1 small mango, peeled, cut from pit, and chopped
6 ice cubes

In a blender, combine all the ingredients and blend until smooth and frothy. Serve immediately.
Makes about 1¹/2 cups (12 fl oz/375 ml); serves 1

Strawberry and Watermelon Booster

This gorgeous drink combines energy from the natural fruit sugar of grapes with the cooling, refreshing properties of watermelon. It also has plenty of vitamin C from the strawberries and the lime. Guarana gives a natural energy boost.

1¹/3 cups (7 oz/220 g) chopped and seeded watermelon flesh
1 cup (4 oz/125 g) hulled fresh, or thawed frozen, strawberries
1 cup (4 oz/125 g) grapes
¹/2 lime, peeled, seeded, and chopped
¹/2 teaspoon guarana powder

In a juicer, process the watermelon, strawberries, grapes, and lime. Whisk in the guarana and serve immediately.
Makes about 1¹/4 cups (10 fl oz/300 ml); serves 1

Cantaloupe and Papaya Juice

Sometimes we may unknowingly be mildly dehydrated, which can cause fatigue. Cantaloupe (rockmelon) has a high water content along with sodium and potassium, which help to rehydrate the body. Papaya aids digestion, chlorophyll promotes red blood cell production, and mint stimulates mental clarity.

¹/4 cantaloupe (rockmelon), peeled, seeded and chopped
¹/2 small papaya, peeled, seeded, and chopped
10 fresh mint leaves
1 teaspoon (or as directed on the bottle) liquid chlorophyll (optional)

In a juicer, alternately process the cantaloupe and papaya with the mint leaves. Stir in the chlorophyll and serve immediately.
Makes about 1¹/2 cups (12 fl oz/375 ml); serves 1

Left: Banana and Mango Frappé

Breakfast in a Glass

For those who can't drink dairy milk, substitute rice or soy milk, but try to use calcium-fortified products. You could also use soy yogurt, though most lactose-intolerant people can tolerate regular yogurt. Almond meal and sunflower seed meal supply unsaturated fatty acids, and wheat germ provides vitamins B and E. If you use a ripe banana, the drink should be sweet enough, but you can add a little honey to taste, if desired.

1 cup (8 fl oz/250 ml) milk
1/2 cup (4 oz/125 g) plain (natural) acidophilus yogurt
1 ripe banana, peeled and chopped
1 cup (4 oz/125 g) hulled fresh, or thawed frozen, strawberries
2 tablespoons almond meal
1 tablespoon sunflower seed meal
2 teaspoons wheat germ

In a blender, combine all the ingredients and process until smooth and frothy. Serve immediately.
Makes about 2 1/2 cups (20 fl oz/625 ml); serves 2

Fig, Plum and Soy Shake

This shake is very thick and filling, and is an ideal breakfast or lunch drink for when you don't have time to sit down and eat. Dried fruits are a great source of concentrated energy, as are nuts and seeds. They are also rich in minerals such as iron and calcium, and the soy milk provides B vitamins and protein.

Right: Breakfast in a Glass

3 dried figs, chopped
3 dried dates, pitted and chopped
3/4 cup (6 fl oz/180 ml) water, plus filtered water to taste
2 red-fleshed plums, pitted and chopped
1 cup (8 fl oz/250 ml) soy milk
1 tablespoon sunflower seed meal
1 tablespoon almond meal

In a small saucepan, combine the figs, dates, and 3/4 cup (6 fl oz/180 ml) water. Bring to a boil, then reduce heat, cover, and simmer until soft, about 10 minutes. Let cool. Transfer to a blender and add the plums, soy milk, and sunflower seed and almond meals. Blend until smooth and frothy. Thin with more water to taste before serving.
Makes about 2 1/2 cups (20 fl oz/625 ml); serves 2

Orange, Pineapple and Mango Juice

The fruits in this drink provide energy in the form of fructose, as well as all the benefits of antioxidants, fiber and vitamins C and B6. The guarana is a natural stimulant.

1 large orange, peeled, seeded, and chopped
1 mango, peeled, cut from pit, and chopped
1/4 pineapple, peeled, cored, and chopped
1/2 teaspoon guarana powder

In a juicer, process the orange, mango, and pineapple. Whisk in the guarana and serve immediately.
Makes about 1 1/4 cups (10 fl oz/300 ml); serves 1

Peach, Apricot and Tahini Blend

This rich, nourishing drink will give you a lift on difficult days. It is high in beta-carotene, calcium, magnesium, and zinc, and the cardamom sweetens the breath, reduces gas, and eases indigestion.

1 large peach, unpeeled, pitted, and chopped
2 fresh figs, chopped
1 cup (8 fl oz/250 ml) apricot nectar
1 tablespoon tahini (sesame paste)
pinch ground cardamom
filtered or spring water to taste (optional)

In a blender, combine all the ingredients except the water and process until smooth. Thin with a small amount of water to taste, if desired.
Makes about 2 cups (16 fl oz/500 ml); serves 2

Carob and Strawberry Milk Shake

This is a great morning or afternoon treat for kids. The strawberries are high in fiber, and have the added benefit of neutralizing plaque, so they help to prevent tooth decay. The carob and almond meal provide protein and calcium, and palm sugar is a slow-release carbohydrate, ensuring sustained energy.

1 cup (4 oz/125 g) hulled fresh, or thawed frozen,
strawberries
3/4 cup (6 fl oz/180 ml) milk
1 tablespoon carob powder
1 tablespoon almond meal
1 1/2 teaspoons palm sugar

In a blender, process all the ingredients until smooth and frothy.
Makes about 1 1/2 cups (12 fl oz/375 ml); serves 1–2

Nectarine, Pineapple and Ginseng Drink

This is great for that mid-afternoon slump. Instead of having a soft drink or coffee, try this truly refreshing drink. It doesn't just taste good, it has beta-carotene and vitamin C, both antioxidants, as well as potassium for healthy blood pressure. The ginseng will boost energy levels, enhance memory, and stimulate the immune system.

1 ginseng tea bag or sachet
1/2 cup (4 fl oz/125 ml) boiling water
1/4 pineapple, peeled, cored, and chopped
1 nectarine, pitted and chopped

Put the ginseng tea bag in a cup and add the boiling water. Let steep for 10 minutes, then remove the tea bag and refrigerate the tea until chilled, about 30 minutes. In a juicer, process the pineapple and nectarine. Pour in the tea and stir to combine.
Makes about 1 1/2 cups (12 fl oz/375 ml); serves 1

Left: Peach, Apricot and Tahini Blend

Pineapple and Coconut Drink

Coconut is very nourishing, particularly to the nervous system. It contains protein, calcium, magnesium, and potassium, to name just a few of the nutrients. Pineapple is rich in vitamins A and C and, along with the mint, it aids digestion.

1/2 pineapple, peeled, cored, and chopped
1/2 cup (4 fl oz/125 ml) coconut milk
6 fresh mint leaves, finely chopped

In a juicer, process the pineapple. Stir in the coconut milk and mint.
Makes about 1 1/2 cups (12 fl oz/375 ml); serves 1

Spinach, Carrot and Orange Juice

Fatigue due to iron deficiency is a common problem in both men and women, and can be particularly noticeable in those switching to a vegetarian diet. This drink has loads of iron, which combined with the vitamin C in the orange, makes it more easily absorbed by the body. Spirulina contains many nutrients, including beta-carotene and vitamin B12, as well as protein.

2 cups (2 oz/60 g) packed fresh spinach leaves
1 carrot, chopped
1 orange, peeled, seeded, and chopped
1/2 teaspoon spirulina powder

In a juicer, process spinach, then the carrot and orange. Whisk in spirulina powder and serve immediately.
Makes about 1 cup (8 fl oz/250 ml); serves 1

Pear and Date Drink

This drink supplies energy from the dates, as well as soluble fiber from the pears, iron from the molasses, and B vitamins from the rice milk.

6 dried dates, pitted and chopped
3/4 cup (6 fl oz/180 ml) water
1 teaspoon blackstrap molasses
2 pears, unpeeled, cored, and chopped
1/2 cup (4 fl oz/125 ml) rice milk

In a small saucepan, combine the dates and water. Bring to a boil, then reduce heat, cover, and simmer until the dates are soft, about 10 minutes. Set aside to cool. In a small bowl, combine 1 tablespoon of the hot date liquid and the molasses; stir until dissolved. In a juicer, process the pears. In a blender, combine the dates and their juice, the dissolved molasses, and rice milk. Process until smooth and frothy.
Makes about 1 cup (8 fl oz/250 ml); serves 1

Right: Pineapple and Coconut Drink

Kiwi and Cantaloupe Juice with Spirulina

This juice is light and refreshing, and provides plenty of vitamins C and A. Spirulina is very rich in nutrients, including protein, iron, calcium, vitamin B12, and beta-carotene. It is also a natural appetite suppressant.

¹/₄ cantaloupe (rockmelon), peeled, seeded, and chopped
2 kiwifruit, peeled and chopped
¹/₂ teaspoon spirulina powder

In a juicer, process the cantaloupe and kiwifruit. Whisk in the spirulina and serve immediately.
Makes about 1 cup (8 fl oz/250 ml); serves 1

Beet and Carrot Juice with Rosemary

This a good drink for anyone who sits at a desk all day. The gingko and rosemary both help to improve circulation and stimulate memory. The beet (beetroot) is high in folic acid, calcium, and iron. Carrots are a rich source of antioxidants in the form of beta-carotene.

1 beet (beetroot), trimmed, unpeeled, and chopped
1 large carrot, chopped
5 ml liquid ginkgo (or as directed on bottle)
¹/₂ teaspoon finely chopped fresh rosemary

In a juicer, process the beet and carrot. Stir in the ginkgo and rosemary. Serve immediately.
Makes about ³/₄ cup (6 fl oz/180 ml); serves 1

Peach and Raisin Smoothie

Kids will enjoy the sweet flavor of this drink, while receiving the benefits of energy from the raisins, protein from the soy milk, and vitamins A and C and zinc from the peaches. Cinnamon improves digestion and stimulates circulation.

¹/₃ cup (2 oz/60 g) golden raisins (sultanas)
2 peaches, unpeeled, pitted, and chopped
1 cup (8 fl oz/250 ml) soy milk
pinch ground cinnamon

Put the raisins in a small bowl and add boiling water to cover. Let stand for 5 minutes, then drain. In a blender, combine the raisins and the remaining ingredients. Process until smooth and frothy.
Makes about 2 cups (8 fl oz/500 ml); serves 2

Left: Kiwi and Cantaloupe Juice with Spirulina

Prune, Honey and Oat Milk Drink

This is a re-energizing and soothing drink for when you are a having a busy, stressful time at work. Oat milk nourishes the nervous system and helps to reduce the effects of stress, yogurt soothes the digestive system, and prunes provide a concentrated source of energy, as well as potassium, iron, and vitamin B6. Saffron is thought to help ease depression.

6 prunes, pitted and chopped
3/4 cup (6 fl oz/180 ml) water
1 teaspoon honey
pinch saffron threads
1 tablespoon hot water
1 cup (8 fl oz/250 ml) oat milk
3/4 cup (6 oz/180 g) apricot acidophilus yogurt

In a small saucepan, combine the prunes and water. Bring to a boil, reduce heat, cover, and simmer until the prunes are soft, about 10 minutes. Let cool. In a small bowl, combine the honey and saffron. Add the hot water and stir to dissolve the honey. Let stand to soften the saffron, about 5 minutes. In a blender, combine the prunes and their liquid, oat milk, yogurt, and saffron liquid. Process until smooth and frothy.
Makes about 2 cups (16 fl oz/500 ml); serves 1–2

Plum, Black Currant and Grape Juice

If you are in the habit of snacking on candy bars when you need an energy boost, try this tangy drink instead. Grapes are high in minerals, including chromium, which helps to prevent sugar cravings. The black currants contain flavonoids, which are antioxidant, and the fennel stimulates the digestive system.

1 large red-fleshed plum, pitted and chopped
1 cup (4 oz/125 g) fresh, or thawed frozen, black currants or blueberries
1 cup (4 oz/125 g) red grapes
1/4 fennel bulb, trimmed, cored, and chopped

In a juicer, process all the ingredients.
Makes about 1 cup (8 fl oz/250 ml); serves 1

Apple and Citrus Juice

Ginseng works to stimulate the mind and body, relieving mental and physical fatigue. Apple and citrus are both good sources of vitamin C, helping to boost the immune system, which can be suppressed when you are overtired.

1 ginseng tea bag or sachet
1/2 cup (4 fl oz/125 ml) boiling water
1 large orange, peeled, seeded, and chopped
1 small lime, peeled, seeded, and chopped
1 apple, unpeeled, cored, and chopped

Put the ginseng tea bag in a cup and add the boiling water. Let steep for 10 minutes, then remove the tea bag and refrigerate the tea until cold, about 20 minutes. In a juicer, process the orange, lime, and apples. Pour in the tea and stir to combine.
Makes about 1 1/4 cups (10 fl oz/300 ml); serves 1

Right: Prune, Honey and Oatmilk Drink

Workout

Exercise is necessary, as it helps maintain a healthy weight, and is recommended to help prevent illness, such as diabetes, heart disease, and even depression. You don't need to be a serious athlete, a simple thirty-minute walk three or four times a week is enough to offset potential problems caused by a sedentary lifestyle.

Whatever your form of exercise and level of intensity, good nutrition is vital to keep your body functioning at peak levels. Those who work harder will have different requirements and demands placed on their body, but generally if you follow basic guidelines you will be supplying your body with adequate nourishment.

This chapter offers drinks that are nutritious and have some specific applications for sports people, but we can't promise they will make you an Olympian! Sports nutrition is a specialized and scientific field, and a professional athlete is guided by their coach and advisers on the appropriate diet for their body type and sport.

Some of our drinks have a high or low glycemic index (GI). This is a measure of how quickly carbohydrate (carbs) foods cause blood sugar levels to rise. Carbs with a low GI cause a gradual rise in blood sugar, offering sustained energy levels. Carbs with a high GI give a quick blood sugar response. This is a new area of nutritional research, and it is yet to be determined how this knowledge can be applied to athletic performance. Put simply, however, you should have carbs with a low GI before an event, to avoid fluctuations in blood sugar, which could interfere with performance. High GI food or drink should be taken after the event to quickly replenish energy levels.

Many drinks on the market are aimed at athletes, with different uses, such as protein drinks for muscle building, or drinks to replace fluids and electrolytes lost through exertion. These drinks are designed for the fairly serious athlete, but are marketed in such a way that the average gym junkie or weekend sports person feels they will improve their performance. Be aware that these drinks can be expensive and contain unnecessary additives. By making your own drinks, you will know exactly what is in them, and will be consuming fresh, nutritious ingredients full of natural vitamins and minerals, with all the enzymes and other compounds needed for your body to make the best use of them.

Pear, Peach and Apricot Juice

This is a good drink to have about 1 hour before a workout. The fruits have a low glycemic index, giving a slow, sustained release of energy.

1 pear, unpeeled, cored, and chopped
1 peach, unpeeled, pitted, and chopped
2 apricots, pitted and chopped
filtered or spring water to taste (optional)

In a juicer, process all the fruit. Thin with a small amount of water, if desired.
Makes about $^3/4$ cup (6 fl oz/180 ml); serves 1

Orange and Broccoli Booster

Broccoli, orange, and kiwifruit are all excellent sources of vitamin C, which is necessary for the production of collagen, a protein needed for maintaining healthy skin, bones, and cartilage. This drink also provides potassium, iron, and vitamin A.

1 large orange, peeled, seeded, and chopped
1 cup (4 oz/125 g) chopped broccoli
1 kiwifruit, peeled and chopped

In a juicer, process all the ingredients.
Makes about 1 cup (8 fl oz/250 ml); serves 1

Banana and Fig Super Smoothie

This thick, filling drink makes an ideal quick breakfast after a morning run or workout. The banana provides potassium for muscle function and carbohydrates to replenish energy stores. The figs provide plenty of potassium, calcium, and magnesium, all needed for healthy bones and muscle function. The milk and whey powder provide protein for muscle building. Flaxseed meal contains essential fatty acids.

4 dried figs, chopped
1 cup (8 fl oz/250 ml) water
1 large, ripe banana, peeled and chopped
1 cup (8 fl oz/250 ml) milk
1 tablespoon flaxseed meal
1 tablespoon protein whey powder

Put the figs in a small saucepan and add the water. Bring to a boil, then reduce heat, cover, and simmer until the figs are soft, about 10 minutes. In a blender, combine the figs and their liquid and all the remaining ingredients. Process until smooth and frothy.
Makes about $1^3/4$ cups (14 fl oz/440 ml); serves 1

Left: Pear, Peach and Apricot Juice

Orange, Cucumber and Parsley Juice

Cucumber is very cooling to the body, so it is useful after an event or workout. The orange supplies vitamin C, which, among other things, helps the body to utilize the iron in the parsley. Spirulina has been dubbed a "superfood" by some alternative therapists, as it is high in so many nutrients.

1 large orange, peeled, seeded and chopped
2 cups (2 oz/60 g) packed parsley sprigs with stems
1 small cucumber, chopped
1/2 teaspoon spirulina powder

In a juicer, process the orange, parsley, and cucumber. Whisk in the spirulina powder.
Makes about 3/4 cup (6 fl oz/180 ml); serves 1

Cantaloupe and Pineapple Recovery Juice

Cantaloupe (rockmelon) and pineapple have a high water content to rehydrate the body. The vitamin C in the pineapple and guava helps to make collagen, an essential protein for healthy bones and cartilage. The enzyme bromelain in pineapple is anti-inflammatory, and aids in the repair of damaged tissue caused by sporting activities.

1/4 cantaloupe (rockmelon), peeled, seeded, and chopped
1/4 pineapple, peeled, cored, and chopped
1 large guava, unpeeled and cut into wedges

In a juicer, process all the ingredients.
Makes about 1 1/2 cups (12 fl oz/375 ml); serves 1

Plum and Berry Blend

This is a refreshing drink. Plums are a good source of potassium, which, along with sodium, balances the fluid and electrolyte balance in cells and tissues. They also contain vitamins A, C and E. Red-fleshed varieties are slightly higher in nutrients than yellow-fleshed ones. The berries provide vitamin C and bioflavonoids, which strengthen veins and arteries.

1 cup (4 oz/125 g) fresh, or thawed frozen, loganberries or blackberries
1 cup (4 oz/125 g) hulled fresh, or thawed frozen, strawberries
3 large red-fleshed plums, pitted and chopped

In a juicer, process all the ingredients.
Makes about 1 cup (8 fl oz/250 ml); serves 1

Right: Orange, Cucumber and Parsley Juice

Pineapple and Papaya Cooler

Whip up this delicious, tangy drink and share it with your workout partner when you get home from the gym. Not only very refreshing, it is loaded with antioxidant vitamins and enzymes. Fennel is a female reproductive tonic and could be useful to female athletes with menstrual problems.

1/2 pineapple, peeled, cored, and chopped
1/4 papaya, peeled, seeded, and chopped
1 lime, peeled, seeded, and chopped
1/4 fennel bulb, trimmed, cored, and chopped

In a juicer, process all the ingredients.
Makes about 2 1/4 cups (18 fl oz/560 ml); serves 2

Banana, Carob and Peanut Butter Smoothie

This filling drink has protein, calcium, iron, potassium, and B vitamins, as well as phosphorus, which helps the body to absorb nutrients. Try it for lunch after a light salad.

1 cup (8 fl oz/250 ml) low-fat milk or fortified soy milk
1 large ripe banana, peeled
2 teaspoons carob powder
1 tablespoon peanut butter
2 teaspoons palm sugar

In a blender, process all the ingredients until smooth.
Makes about 1 1/2 cups (12 fl oz/375 ml); serves 1

Left: Pineapple and Papaya Cooler

Pear and Almond Shake

Pears are a good source of energy because of their natural fruit sugars; they also provide potassium and fiber. Milk supplies calcium, while almonds also have minerals needed for strong bones. Flaxseed oil is a good source of essential fatty acids, which, among other things, work to control inflammatory reactions. Glucosamine is used by the body to repair damaged cartilage and to strengthen joints.

5 oz (150 g) canned pear halves in natural juice, drained
1 cup (8 fl oz/250 ml) milk
2 tablespoons almond meal
2 teaspoons flaxseed oil, or as directed on package (optional)
1 teaspoon glucosamine powder, or as directed on package (optional)

In a blender, combine all the ingredients and process until smooth and frothy.
Makes about 2 cups (16 fl oz/500 ml); serves 1–2

Melon, Grape and Lychee Juice

Melon and lychees are very cooling to the body, so this is a good drink to have after a workout. Grapes replenish energy fast because they have a fairly high glycemic index.

¹/₂ small honeydew melon, peeled, seeded, and chopped
1 cup (4 oz/125 g) grapes
6 lychees, peeled and seeded

In a juicer, process all the ingredients.
Makes about 1 cup (8 fl oz/250 ml); serves 1

Grapefruit, Papaya and Mango Juice

Papaya and mango have a high glycemic index, so this is a good drink to quickly restore energy after exercise.

1 ruby grapefruit, peeled, seeded, and chopped
¹/₄ papaya, peeled, seeded, and chopped
1 mango, peeled, cut from pit, and chopped

In a juicer, process all the ingredients.
Makes about 1 cup (8 fl oz/250 ml); serves 1

Carrot, Orange and Ginger Juice

This drink fits in well with a healthy lifestyle. Ginseng gives a natural energy boost, and carrot and orange contain the important antioxidants vitamins C and A. Ginger helps to stimulate circulation and aids digestion.

1 ginseng tea bag or sachet
¹/₂ cup (4 fl oz/125 ml) boiling water
1 large carrot, chopped
1 large orange, peeled, seeded, and chopped
¹/₂-inch (12-mm) piece fresh ginger

Put the ginseng tea bag in a cup and add the boiling water. Let steep for 10 minutes, then remove the tea bag and refrigerate the tea until cold, about 20 minutes. In a juicer, process the carrot, orange, and ginger. Pour in the tea and stir to combine.
Makes about 1¹/₄ cups (10 fl oz/300 ml); serves 1

Right: Melon, Grape and Lychee Juice

Apricot and Brazil Blend

This tangy drink provides plenty of iron from the dried apricots, vitamin C from the oranges, and vitamin E from the wheat germ. Brazil nuts contain selenium, a mineral that is an antioxidant and helps with growth, fertility, and healthy thyroid function.

1/4 cup (1 1/2 oz/45 g) dried apricots
1 cup (8 fl oz/250 ml) water, plus filtered
or spring cold water to taste
juice of 2 large oranges
6 Brazil nuts
1 tablespoon wheat germ

In a small saucepan, combine the dried apricots and water. Bring to a boil, reduce heat, cover, and simmer for 10 minutes; let cool. In a blender, combine the apricots and their liquid, and all remaining ingredients except the cold water and process until smooth. Thin with cold water to desired consistency.
Makes about 1 1/4 cups (10 fl oz/300 ml); serves 1

Peach and Ginger Thick Shake

This drink could be good as part of a meal in a healthy eating program, perhaps served after a salad for lunch. L-carnitine powder works to metabolize fat and to convert it into energy, peaches contain antioxidants, and ginger improves digestion.

2 large peaches, peeled, pitted, and chopped
1/2 cup (4 oz/125 g) low-fat plain (natural) acidophilus
yogurt or soy yogurt
1 cup (8 fl oz/250 ml) low-fat milk or fortified soy milk,
chilled
2 teaspoons honey
pinch ground ginger
1 teaspooon L-carnitine powder, or as directed (optional)

In a food processor, combine all the ingredients and process until smooth and frothy.
Makes about 2 cups (16 fl oz/500 ml); serves 1–2

Tomato and Cabbage Revitalizer

This vegetable drink is good to have after exercise. The cabbage, celery, and tomatoes contain potassium and a little sodium, needed to balance electrolytes. Celery also has anti-inflammatory properties, useful in cases of injury or discomfort.

1 ripe tomato, cut into wedges
1 1/3 cups (4 oz/125 g) chopped cabbage
1 cup (1 oz/30 g) packed parsley sprigs with stems
2 celery stalks

In a juicer, process all the ingredients.
Makes about 1 cup (8 fl oz/250 ml); serves 1

Left: Apricot and Brazil Blend

Stress and Relaxation

This chapter has drinks with several different applications. Some have calming properties that reduce anxiety, helping you to function well during a busy day or stressful situation. Others have a sedative effect, useful if you are having trouble sleeping but do not want to resort to drugs. Some of the drinks are nonalcoholic replacements for cocktails. Some are warming, some are cooling, but all of them will help you feel better.

Stress seems to be the buzzword of the times. Everyone is busy, overworked, "stressed out," and there are so many factors contributing to this. There is pressure from our jobs, relationship and family problems, money worries, life changes, and losses to deal with.

Stress is a physical condition, originally important and healthy for the human race, as part of our survival instinct. In primitive times, a rush of the hormone adrenaline in response to a "fight or flight" situation facilitated a quick response. Adrenaline causes physical changes that are useful if you are threatened by a wild animal, but modern humans experience the same physical responses with no physical release. Combined with other factors, such as poor diet and lack of exercise, the stress that was designed to help us survive can be a life-threatening problem. Stress can contribute to heart disease and strokes, and can suppress the immune system leaving the body susceptible to illness.

There are several ways of dealing with stress. Exercise is good, as it simulates the original use for adrenaline—try running, fast walking, or a sport you like. The physical release is fast and effective, releasing endorphins, which make you feel good, and take your mind off problems. A more passive approach is to learn relaxation techniques, such as yoga, meditation, breathing, or positive visualization.

Maximum nutrition is one of the best ways to deal with stress. An increased supply of B vitamins, vitamin C, and zinc helps the body to cope with the extra demands placed on it, and boost the immune system. Eat nourishing meals and avoid fatty, hard-to-digest foods. Cut down on stimulants, such as coffee, soft drinks, alcohol, and cigarettes, which deplete nutrients and lead to further anxiety. As well as coping with stress, look for ways to reduce it. Deal with problems and resolve conflict as it arises, as delaying often causes more stress in the long term.

Mulled Rose Hip Tea

A tasty and warming drink for a cold winter day. Rose hip tea is an excellent source of vitamin C, and the cinnamon stimulates circulation.

1 rose hip tea bag
1 cup (8 fl oz/250 ml) boiling water
1 cinnamon stick
1 strip orange zest, 1-inch (2.5-cm) wide
1 teaspoon honey

Put the tea bag in a cup and add the boiling water. Add the cinnamon stick and orange zest and let steep for 5 minutes. Remove the tea bag, cinnamon stick, and orange zest, and stir in the honey.
Makes about 1 cup (8 fl oz/250 ml); serves 1

Watermelon Cooler

If you are having a busy day and are feeling hot and bothered, try this cooling, soothing drink. All the ingredients have cooling properties and are very hydrating.

2 cups (10 oz/300 g) chopped and seeded watermelon flesh
1 small cucumber, chopped
few drops rose water to taste (optional)

In a juicer, process the watermelon and cucumber. Add rose water to taste, if desired, and stir to combine.
Makes about 1 cup (8 fl oz/250 ml); serves 1

Warm Spiced Milk

It's not just an old wives' tale—warm milk really does help you to fall asleep. Milk contains the amino acid tryptophan, which is converted in the body to serotonin, helping to induce sleep. The cardamom and nutmeg are also soothing and sleep inducing.

1 cup (8 fl oz/250 ml) milk
pinch ground cardamom
pinch ground nutmeg

Put the milk in a small saucepan and heat over low heat until warm. Pour into a cup, add the spices, and stir to combine.
Makes about 1 cup (8 fl oz/250 ml); serves 1

Left: Mulled Rose Hip Tea

Peach and Raspberry Cocktail

A lovely nonalcoholic cocktail to sip on a warm summer evening.

2 ripe, juicy peaches, peeled, pitted, and chopped
1 cup (4 oz/125 g) fresh, or thawed frozen, raspberries
sparkling mineral water to taste

In a blender, puree the peaches and raspberries until smooth. Press through a fine-mesh sieve to remove the raspberry seeds. Pour into 2 tall glasses, then gradually add the mineral water to your prefered consistency. Stir gently to combine.
Makes about 1³/4 cups (14 fl oz/440 ml); serves 2

Warm Apple and Chamomile Drink

Chamomile tea is very relaxing and helps to reduce anxiety. The apples and vanilla add delicious flavors.

1 chamomile tea bag
¹/2 cup (4 fl oz/125 ml) boiling water
2 apples, unpeeled, cored, and chopped
1 teaspoon honey
3 drops vanilla extract

Put the tea bag in a cup and add the boiling water. Let steep for 5 minutes then remove the tea bag. In a juicer, process the apples. Stir the apple juice, honey, and vanilla into the warm tea.
Makes about ³/4 cup (6 fl oz/180 ml); serves 1

Strawberry Soother

Valerian is a sedative herb that calms the nerves and induces sleep. Lettuce also has calming, sedative properties.

1 valerian tea bag
¹/2 cup (4 fl oz/125 ml) boiling water
1 cup (4 oz/125 g) hulled fresh, or thawed frozen, strawberries
1¹/3 cups (4 oz/125 g) choppped iceberg lettuce

Put the tea bag in a cup and add the boiling water. Let steep for 10 minutes, then remove the tea bag and refrigerate the tea until cold, about 20 minutes. In a juicer, process the strawberries and lettuce. Pour in the tea and stir to combine.
Makes about 1 cup (8 fl oz/250 ml); serves 1

Right: Peach and Raspberry Cocktail

Pineapple, Ginger and Lemon Juice

This drink tastes great and has a real kick. The pineapple has enzymes which stimulate digestion, and, like the lemon, it also contains vitamin C. Ginger also stimulates digestion.

1/2 pineapple, peeled, cored, and chopped
1/2-inch (12-mm) piece fresh ginger
1/2 lemon, peeled and seeded

In a juicer, process all the ingredients.
Makes about 1 1/4 cups (10 fl oz/300 ml); serves 1

Tomato and Basil Aperitif

Choose beautifully ripe tomatoes for the best flavor, and optimum nutrients. This is a great before-dinner drink, as pepper stimulates the appetite. Basil complements the flavors of the tomato, and has the added benefit of boosting the immune system.

8 large basil leaves
3 ripe tomatoes, chopped
1 small cucumber, chopped
freshly ground black pepper to taste

In a juicer, alternately process the basil with the tomato, then the cucumber. Stir to combine. Season with the pepper.
Makes about 1 1/2 cups (12 fl oz/375 ml); serves 1–2

Warming Apricot Smoothie

This is a nourishing, relaxing drink to have when you want to wind down. The dried apricots are rich in beta-carotene, iron, and potassium, and the warm milk is slightly sedative.

1/3 cup (2 oz/60 g) dried apricots
1 cup (8 fl oz/250 ml) water
3/4 cup (6 fl oz/185 ml) milk
pinch ground ginger
1 teaspoon honey, or to taste

In a small saucepan, combine the dried apricots and water. Bring to a boil, reduce heat, cover, and simmer for 10 minutes; let cool slightly. In a small saucepan, heat the milk until bubbles form around the edge of the pan. In a blender, combine the apricots and their liquid, the milk, ginger, and honey. Process until smooth and drink warm.
Makes about 1 1/4 cups (10 fl oz/300 ml); serves 1

Left: Pineapple, Ginger and Lemon Juice

Tropical Colada

This delicious and nutritious drink is great for when you don't want to drink alcohol at a party.

1 mango, peeled, cut from pit, and chopped
1/4 pineapple, peeled, cored, and chopped
ice cubes
1/2 cup (4 fl oz/125 ml) coconut milk

In a juicer, process the mango and pineapple until smooth. Put a few ice cubes into 2 tall glasses and pour the juice over. Add the coconut milk and stir to combine. Serve immediately.
Makes about 1³/4 cups (14 fl oz/440 ml); serves 2

Melon-Berry Crush

This pretty, summery drink is very refreshing and rehydrating. Strawberries are thought to have calming properties.

1¹/2 cups (8 oz/250 g) chopped and seeded watermelon flesh
1/4 cantaloupe (rockmelon), peeled, seeded, and chopped
1 cup (4 oz/125 g) hulled fresh, or thawed frozen, strawberries
ice cubes

In a blender, combine all the fruits and process until smooth. Serve immediately over ice.
Makes about 2 cups (16 fl oz/500 ml); serves 2

Soothing Citrus Iced Tea

Lemon balm calms the nervous system, helps you to sleep, and eases indigestion.

1 lemon balm tea bag
1 cup (8 fl oz/250 ml) boiling water
3–4 ice cubes
juice of 1 large orange
6 fresh mint leaves, finely chopped

Put the lemon balm tea bag in a cup and add the boiling water. Let steep for 10 minutes, then remove the tea bag and refrigerate the tea until chilled, about 30 minutes. Put the ice cubes in a tall glass, and add the orange juice and tea. Stir in the mint leaves.
Makes about 1¹/2 cups (12 fl oz/375 ml); serves 1

Right: Tropical Colada

Tonics and Remedies

Some of the drinks in this chapter may not be as tasty as other drinks in the book, mainly because they contain combinations of ingredients that are used for specific conditions. If you are looking for some relief from say, diarrhea or menstrual cramping, then you probably won't be too concerned about flavor. Think of these drinks as medicinal.

Remember that taking care of your health is an ongoing concern, and if you can maintain a good level of health, then minor ailments will not usually occur, or they will be less severe. Neglecting your health, then looking for a quick fix at a time of crisis is not the way to go. Eating sensibly, exercising regularly, taking time out to relax, and getting enough sleep are the keys to staying well.

Foods, herbs, and spices have long been the first line of defense in treating illnesses, both as a general preventative and for their specific medicinal qualities. Prunes are well known for their laxative properties, and of course there is that old saying, "an apple a day keeps the doctor away." It is interesting to note how many old-time remedies have a solid scientific basis, even though they were used long before the reasons for their medicinal value was known. Cranberries are a good example. Native to North America, they have been used for centuries as a folk remedy. They are best known now as an effective cure and preventative for urinary tract infections such as cystitis, though recent research has found many other benefits from these antibacterial properties, such as treating gastric ulcers and gum disease.

Ginger is an herb that has been used for hundreds of years to treat nausea. It is just as relevant today, particularly in the case of morning sickness, where drugs cannot be taken, as it is very safe and effective.

Note that the drinks in this chapter can be used to help ease particular ailments or conditions, but they are in no way meant to replace advice and treatment from a health-care professional.

Cranberry, Pear and Lime Juice

(urinary tract infections)

Cranberries are a very effective and fast-working solution to urinary tract infections. They are tart in flavor, while commercial juices are often high in sugar. Here, the pear provides sweetness, while the lime contributes vitamin C.

1 cup (4 oz/125 g) fresh, or thawed frozen, cranberries
1 pear, unpeeled, cored, and chopped
$^1/_2$ lime, peeled, seeded, and chopped

In a juicer, process all the ingredients.
Makes about $^3/4$ cup (6 fl oz/180 ml); serves 1

Fennel, Parsley and Apricot Juice

(menstrual cramping and bloating)

Fennel is a female reproductive tonic and, along with parsley, is a diuretic that helps to counteract water retention and therefore reduce bloating. Parsley also provides magnesium to reduce muscle cramping. The apricots provide some iron, and the orange helps the body to absorb the iron from the parsley.

$^1/_2$ fennel bulb, trimmed, cored, and chopped
2 cups (2 oz/60 g) packed parsley sprigs with stems
2 fresh apricots, pitted, and chopped
1 orange, peeled, seeded, and chopped

In a juicer, process all the ingredients.
Makes about $^3/4$ cup (6 fl oz/180 ml); serves 1

Apricot and Bilberry Juice

(eye tonic)

Eyesight tends to deteriorate with age, but this drink may help to prevent and rectify the problem. Bilberries are rich in anthocyanidins, which promote clear vision. If you can't find them, use blueberries, which have similar, though not quite as potent, properties. Both carrots and apricots have vitamin A, which contributes to healthy eyesight. The antihistamines in cilantro help to alleviate allergic irritation in the eyes.

2 apricots, pitted and chopped
1 cup (4 oz/125 g) fresh, or thawed frozen, bilberries or blueberries
$^1/_2$ cup ($^1/_2$ oz/15 g) cilantro (fresh coriander) sprigs with stems
1 carrot, chopped

In a juicer, process all the ingredients.
Makes about $^1/2$ cup (4 fl oz/125 ml); serves 1

Left: Cranberry, Pear and Lime Juice

Kiwi Cold Fighter

(colds)

This drink is packed with vitamin C from the fruit, while the ginger and cayenne will help to warm the body and clear the sinuses.

2 kiwifruit, peeled and chopped
1/4 pineapple, peeled, cored, and chopped
1 orange, peeled, seeded, and chopped (white pith left on)
1/2-inch (12-mm) piece fresh ginger
pinch cayenne pepper

In a juicer, process the kiwifruit, pineapple, orange, and ginger. Whisk in the cayenne and serve immediately.
Makes about 1¹/4 cups (10 fl oz/300 ml); serves 1

Celery and Apple Juice

(arthritis)

Celery and fenugreek both have anti-inflammatory properties, while strawberries contain a natural aspirin-like substance to relieve pain.

1 fenugreek tea bag
1/2 cup (4 fl oz/125 ml) boiling water
2 stalks celery, chopped
1 apple, unpeeled, cored, and chopped
1 cup (4 oz/125 g) hulled fresh, or thawed frozen,
strawberries

Put the tea bag in a cup and add the boiling water. Let steep for 10 minutes, then remove the tea bag and refrigerate the tea until cold, about 15 minutes. In a juicer, process the celery, apple, and strawberries. Stir the juice into the tea.
Makes about 1 cup (8 fl oz/250 ml); serves 1

Left: Kiwi Cold Fighter

Grapefruit, Lemon and Ginger Juice

(appetite stimulant)

This tart drink will enliven any jaded appetite. The grapefruit and lemon are both appetite stimulants, as is the ginger. The added bonus is lots of vitamin C, and soluble fiber.

½ ruby grapefruit, peeled, seeded, and chopped
1 small lemon, peeled, seeded, and chopped
½-inch (12-mm) piece fresh ginger
1 apple, peeled, cored, and chopped

In a juicer, process all the ingredients.
Makes about 1 cup (8 fl oz/250 ml); serves 1

Apple, Prune and Aloe Juice

(constipation)

This is a very effective drink if you are suffering from constipation. Prunes are laxative, while the apple provides soluble fiber. Aloe vera juice soothes the gastro-intestinal tract, and is also gently laxative. Psyllium husks create soft bulk.

⅓ cup (2 oz/60 g) pitted prunes, chopped
1 cup (8 fl oz/250 ml) water
2 apples, peeled, cored, and chopped
1 tablespoon aloe vera juice, or as directed
2 teaspoons psyllium husks

In a small saucepan, combine the prunes and water. Bring to a boil, reduce heat, cover, and simmer for 10 minutes. Let cool. In a juicer, process the apples. In a blender, combine apple juice, prunes and aloe vera juice. Process until smooth. Whisk in the psyllium husks and serve immediately.
Makes about 1¼ cups (10 fl oz/300 ml); serves 1

Melon Mouth Healer

(mouth ulcers)

Mouth ulcers seem minor but they make life so unpleasant—they hurt when you eat and talk. They can be caused by many different things including allergies, deficiencies, stress, or just being tired and run-down. The slippery elm in this drink soothes the mouth, the sunflower seed meal provides zinc, and the cabbage has healing properties.

¼ honeydew melon, peeled, seeded, and chopped
1 cup (3 oz/90 g) chopped cabbage
2 teaspoons slippery elm powder
1 tablespoon sunflower seed meal

In a juicer, process the melon and cabbage. Whisk in the slippery elm powder and the sunflower seed meal. Sip the drink slowly.
Makes about 1 cup (8 fl oz/250 ml); serves 1

Right: Grapefruit, Lemon and Ginger Juice

Tomato Tonic

(hangover)

There isn't really a cure for a hangover, but this tonic may help. The tomatoes, pepper, and lemon all replenish vitamin C, and the brewer's yeast supplies B vitamins.

2 large ripe tomatoes, chopped
1 red bell pepper (capsicum), seeded and chopped
1 lemon, peeled, seeded, and chopped
1 teaspoon brewer's yeast

In a juicer, process the tomatoes, bell pepper, and lemon. Whisk in the brewer's yeast and serve immediately.
Makes about 1^{1}/4 cups (10 fl oz/300 ml); serves 1

Pineapple and Grape Juice

(weight loss)

This drink can aid in a weight-loss program, as the pineapple is a natural appetite suppressant, while spirulina expands in the stomach to create a feeling of fullness. The grapes help to reduce food cravings by balancing blood sugar.

^{1}/4 pineapple, peeled, cored, and chopped
1 cup (4 oz/125 g) grapes
1 teaspoon spirulina powder

In a juicer, process the pineapple and grapes. Whisk in the spirulina and serve immediately.
Makes about ^{3}/4 cup (6 fl oz/180 ml); serves 1

Fennel and Mint Drink

(gas)

Fennel, mint, and chamomile tea all work to reduce and relieve gas and the discomfort caused by it.

1 chamomile tea bag
^{3}/4 cup (6 fl oz/180 ml) boiling water
1 small fennel bulb, trimmed, cored, and chopped
6 fresh mint leaves, finely chopped

Put the tea bag in a cup and add the boiling water. Let steep for 10 minutes, then remove the tea bag and refrigerate the tea until cold, about 20 minutes. In a juicer, process the fennel. Stir the juice into the tea, then add the mint and stir to combine.
Makes about 1 cup (8 fl oz/250 ml); serves 1

Right: Tomato Tonic

Orange and Herb Brew

(cough)

This drink helps if you are suffering from a cough connected with a cold. Thyme works as an expectorant, while sage and honey ease a sore throat. Garlic has antiviral and antibacterial properties and the orange supplies vitamin C. Echinacea is an herb that works to strengthen the immune system.

2 large fresh thyme sprigs
6 fresh sage leaves, coarsely chopped
1 cup (8 fl oz/250 ml) boiling water
1 teaspoon honey
1 small garlic clove, finely chopped
juice of 1 large orange
liquid echinacea, as directed on bottle (optional)

In a cup, combine the thyme and sage and add the boiling water. Let steep for 5 minutes. Stir in the honey and garlic and let stand for another 5 minutes. Strain the liquid and stir in the orange juice and echinacea.
Makes about 1 cup (8 fl oz/250 ml); serves 1

Ginger and Coriander Seed Tea

(morning sickness)

Ginger is very soothing to the stomach and is a well-known remedy for nausea. Coriander seeds aid digestion, helping to settle the stomach after eating.

1/2-inch (12-mm) piece fresh ginger, finely sliced
1 teaspoon coriander seeds
1 cup (8 fl oz/250 ml) boiling water

In a small teapot, combine the ginger and coriander seeds. Add the boiling water, and let steep for 5 minutes. Pour through a small sieve into a cup. Sip slowly.
Makes 1 cup (8 fl oz/250 ml); serves 1

Left: Orange and Herb Brew

Guava and Rice Milk Blend

(diarrhea)

Nutmeg and guava both have diarrhea-easing properties, while rice milk is a nourishing, soothing fluid. The acidophilus yogurt helps to normalize the bacteria in the bowel.

1 large guava, unpeeled and chopped
1/2 cup (4 fl oz/125 ml) rice milk
1/2 cup (4 oz/125 g) acidophilus yogurt
pinch ground nutmeg

In a juicer, process the guava. In a blender, combine the guava juice and all the remaining ingredients and process until smooth.
Makes about 1 1/4 cups (10 fl oz/300 ml); serves 1

Strawberry and Rose Hip Skin Tonic

(complexion)

There are millions of products on the market that claim to beautify your skin from the outside, but it is what we put inside our bodies that really counts. Strawberries and rose hip tea are both good sources of vitamin C, needed for the production of collagen to promote healthy skin. The apple provides soluble fiber, and the chlorophyll gives a concentrated nutrient boost and an internal cleanse.

1 rose hip tea bag
3/4 cup (6 fl oz/185 ml) boiling water
1 cup (4 oz/125 g) hulled fresh, or thawed frozen, strawberries
1 apple, unpeeled, cored, and chopped
1 teaspoon liquid chlorophyll, or as directed (optional)

Put the tea bag in a cup and add the boiling water. Let steep for 10 minutes, then remove the tea bag and refrigerate the tea until it is cold, about 15 minutes. In a juicer, process the strawberries and apple. Stir the juice into the tea, then add the chlorophyll and stir to combine.
Makes about 1 1/2 cups (12 fl oz/375 ml); serves 1

Right: Guava and Rice Milk Blend

Immunity and Prevention

As we go about our daily life, we are constantly exposed to bacteria, viruses, and all kinds of germs that may or may not make us sick. A strong immune system is the best defense you have against potential disease. Prevention is much better than cure, as anyone who has suffered a serious illness can tell you.

Nutrition plays a huge role in keeping the immune system working properly. A balanced diet of fresh fruit and vegetables, whole grains, legumes, nuts, seeds, dairy products, and meat (unless vegetarian) should fill all your nutritional requirements. Avoid nutrient-poor foods and beverages such as fast foods, chips, candy, and soft drinks. These things fill you up without contributing anything in the way of the vitamins or minerals needed for sustenance, and these food items are usually full of fats that can contribute to obesity and related problems, such as heart disease and diabetes.

You may have heard that moderate amounts of alcohol can primarily play a part in preventing heart disease and that drinking one or two small glasses of red wine per day can contribute antioxidant benefits. There are many sources of antioxidants—you do not need to get them from wine. Alcohol is high in calories, without providing many nutrients, and in fact can deplete stores of certain nutrients. Heavy drinking is harmful to the liver in the long term, leading to serious disease. Even if you are a light drinker, try to have at least two alcohol-free days per week. Also, avoid smoking and passive smoking.

Exercise, of course, goes hand in hand with a good diet. Exercise does much more than just keep your muscles limber—it helps to lower cholesterol, prevent and reduce obesity, prevent diabetes, improve circulation, lift your mood, and increase strength and fitness. Recent findings show that exercising with hand weights and pursuing other weight-bearing activities can help to prevent osteoporosis by increasing bone density. This kind of exercise can be taken up at any age, with professional advice.

Emotions also have an impact on the immune system. Depression, stress, anxiety, and unhappiness can all contribute to a weaker immune response. Take steps to alleviate those problems that cause negative feelings, or try relaxation techniques like massage, meditation, or yoga to help you deal with them.

Mango Mix

This juice is brimful of beta-carotene and vitamin C, two powerful antioxidants that help to prevent cancer and premature aging, and also boost the immune system.

1 mango, peeled, cut from pit, and chopped
1/4 pineapple, peeled, cored, and chopped
1/4 papaya, peeled, seeded, and chopped
1/2 lime, peeled, seeded, and chopped

In a juicer, process all the ingredients.
Makes about 2 cups (16 fl oz/500 ml); serves 2

Orange and Ginger Juice

The ginger in this juice helps to stimulate poor circulation, while the orange and cantaloupe (rockmelon) have lots of vitamins A and C to boost the immune system. The bioflavanoids in the orange pith help to guard against viruses and bacteria, so leave as much on as you can when peeling.

2 oranges, peeled, seeded, and chopped
1/4 cantaloupe (rockmelon), peeled, seeded, and chopped
1/2-inch (12-mm) piece fresh ginger

In a juicer, process all the ingredients.
Makes about 1³/4 cups (14 fl oz/440 ml); serves 1–2

Tomato and Watercress Juice

Tomatoes are rich in the carotenoid lycopene, which may help to prevent prostate cancer. Use perfectly ripe, deep red tomatoes, because as well as having the best flavor, they will have a higher level of lycopene. Watercress is a member of the crucifer family of vegetables (that includes broccoli and cabbage) and has cancer-preventing benefits, particularly for the colon and bladder. It is rich in vitamin C, beta-carotene, and contains some vitamin E.

2 large, ripe tomatoes, chopped
1 bunch watercress, with stems
1/2 lemon, peeled, seeded, and chopped

In a juicer, process all the ingredients.
Makes about ³/4 cup (6 fl oz/180 ml); serves 1

Left: Mango Mix

Carrot and Orange Juice

This is good if you feel a cold coming on. Leave as much of the white pith on the orange as you can when peeling it, as it contains bioflavonoids that help provide immunity against bacteria and viruses. The ginger helps to protect against respiratory infections, while sage is antiseptic and is traditionally used to treat sore throats.

1 carrot, chopped
1 orange, peeled, seeded, and chopped
1/2-inch (12-mm) piece fresh ginger
10 fresh sage leaves, finely chopped

In a juicer, process the carrot, orange, and ginger. Stir in the sage.
Makes about 3/4 cup (6 fl oz/180 ml); serves 1

Wheatgrass Booster

Wheatgrass juice has a long list of nutritional benefits. It helps detoxify and regenerate the liver and blood, and provides vitamins, minerals, enzymes, and amino acids. Unfortunately, domestic juicers aren't able to produce wheatgrass juice, so look in the refrigerator of natural foods stores for a bottle. Always check the label, as the juice must be consumed within 36 hours of being made.

2 apples, peeled, cored, and chopped
2 tablespoons wheatgrass juice

In a juicer, process the apples. Stir in the wheatgrass juice and serve immediately.
Makes about 1 cup (8 fl oz/250 ml); serves 1

Banana Bone Builder

Calcium levels need to be replenished daily to prevent osteoporosis in later life. This drink provides plenty of calcium, from the milk, tahini, carob, and almonds. It also contains magnesium and phosphorus, both of which work with calcium to help prevent bone deterioration.

1 large ripe banana, peeled
1 tablespoon almond meal
1 tablespoon tahini (sesame paste)
1 cup (8 fl oz/250 ml) low-fat milk
1/2 tablespoon carob powder
1 teaspoon honey (optional)

In a blender, combine all the ingredients and process until smooth and frothy.
Makes about 1 1/2 cups (12 fl oz/375 ml); serves 1

Right: Carrot and Orange Juice

Spinach and Orange Juice

Spinach is rich in antioxidants, which slow cell degeneration, as well as being high in calcium, folic acid, and vitamin A. The pectin in the orange helps to lower blood cholesterol levels, and its vitamin C aids in fighting off bacterial infections. Spirulina is a rich source of many vitamins and minerals, including vitamin B12, which can be lacking in a vegetarian diet.

2 cups (2 oz/60 g) fresh spinach leaves
1 large orange, peeled, seeded, and chopped
1/2 teaspoon spirulina powder

In a juicer, process the spinach and orange. Whisk in the spirulina and serve immediately.
Makes about 1 1/4 cups (10 fl oz/300 ml); serves 1.

Red Pepper, Carrot and Celery Juice

The old legend that carrots are good for your eyesight is true. The beta-carotene in the carrots converts to vitamin A in the body to maintain healthy vision. The red pepper is also a good source of beta-carotene, as well as vitamin C. Celery is a mild diuretic and contains eight known anti-cancer compounds.

1 large red bell pepper (capsicum), seeded and chopped
1 large carrot, chopped
2 stalks celery, chopped

In a juicer, process all the ingredients.
Makes about 1 cup (8 fl oz/250 ml); serves 1

Apple and Alfalfa Juice

This is a good drink for those worried about cholesterol. The apple supplies pectin, a soluble fiber, which reduces the levels of cholesterol in the blood. Lecithin helps to break down and eliminate cholesterol, and works to prevent gallstones. Alfalfa also lowers cholesterol and provides many other nutrients.

2 oz (60 g) alfalfa sprouts
1 apple, unpeeled, cored, and chopped
1 pear, unpeeled, cored, and chopped
1 teaspoon lecithin

In a juicer, process first the alfalfa, then the apple and pear. Whisk in the lecithin, though it will not completely dissolve.
Makes about 1 cup (8 fl oz/250 ml); serves 1

Left: Spinach and Orange Juice

Beet and Broccoli Juice

This earthy-flavored drink packs a wallop of nutrients and has cancer-preventing properties. Make this whenever you feel you need a strong nutritional boost.

1 beet (beetroot), trimmed, unpeeled, and chopped
1 cup (4 oz/125 g) chopped broccoli
1 large tomato, chopped

In a juicer, process all the ingredients.
Makes about 1 cup (8 fl oz/250 ml); serves 1

Super-C Juice

These fruits are all high in vitamin C, so this juice is a good preventative in cold and flu season. When peeling the grapefruit and orange, leave on as much of the white pith as you can to preserve the antibacterial and antiviral bioflavonoids it contains.

1 grapefruit, peeled, seeded, and chopped
1 large orange, peeled, seeded, and chopped
1 kiwifruit, peeled and chopped

In a juicer, process all the ingredients.
Makes about 1 cup (8 fl oz/250 ml); serves 1

Strawberry Shake

A good drink for people who have just quit smoking. The oat milk has properties that bind to nicotine receptors in the lungs, reducing withdrawal symptoms. Strawberries replenish the vitamin C depleted by smoking, which works with the vitamin E in the wheat germ to eliminate the free radicals caused by cigarette smoke. The cinnamon stimulates circulation, which is impaired by smoking.

1 cup (8 fl oz/250 ml) oat milk
1 cup (4 oz/125 g) hulled fresh, or thawed frozen,
strawberries
1 tablespoon wheat germ
pinch ground cinnamon
1 teaspoon honey

In a blender, combine all the ingredients and blend until smooth and frothy. Serve immediately.
Makes about 1¹/2 cups (12 fl oz/375 ml); serves 1

Right: Beet and Broccoli Juice

Melon and Mint Juice

This drink helps when you are feeling hot and flustered. Melon and cucumber both have a high water content and are therefore very cooling and hydrating. Mint is a cooling herb that helps to stimulate mental clarity.

15 fresh mint leaves
1/2 small honeydew melon, peeled, seeded, and chopped
1 small cucumber, chopped

In a juicer, alternately process the mint leaves with pieces of melon, then cucumber.
Makes about 2 cups (16 fl oz/500 ml); serves 2

Papaya and Pineapple Juice

This is a good drink for those troubled by digestive problems. The pineapple contains the enzyme bromelain and the papaya contains the enzyme papain, both of which work to stimulate the digestive system. The apple provides fiber in the form of pectin, and the astringency of the lemon stimulates the liver.

1/2 small papaya, peeled, seeded, and chopped
1/2 small pineapple, peeled, cored, and chopped
1 large apple, unpeeled, cored, and chopped
1/2 lemon, peeled, seeded, and chopped

In a juicer, process all the ingredients.
Makes about 2 cups (16 fl oz/250 ml); serves 2

Sesame-Bok Choy Blend

This drink provides plenty of calcium for those looking for an alternative to dairy foods. Bok choy and broccoli are great vegetable sources of calcium, and they also have cancer-preventing properties. The vitamin C in the lemon juice will help the body to utilize the iron in the green vegetables.

1 cup (4 oz/125 g) chopped broccoli
1 bunch baby bok choy
1 carrot, chopped
1/2 lemon, peeled, seeded, and chopped
1 tablespoon tahini (sesame paste)

In a juicer, process the broccoli, bok choy, carrot, and lemon. Pour the juice into a blender and add the tahini. Process briefly until combined, and serve immediately.
Makes about 1 cup (8 fl oz/250 ml); serves 1

Left: Melon and Mint Juice

Berry and Orange Juice

The berries in this drink combine to strengthen the arteries, veins, and capillaries, and the ginger promotes blood circulation. Blueberries and cranberries are also useful for bladder problems, and the orange zest contributes bioflavonoids.

1 cup (4 oz/125 g) fresh, or thawed frozen, blueberries
1 cup (4 oz/125 g) fresh, or thawed frozen, cranberries
1 cup (4 oz/125 g) hulled fresh, or thawed frozen, strawberries
1/2-inch (12-mm) piece fresh ginger
2 teaspoons finely grated orange zest

In a juicer, process the berries and ginger. Whisk in the orange zest.
Makes about 3/4 cup (6 fl oz/180 ml); serves 1

Citrus Immunity Booster

Echinacea is a herb that helps to boost the immune system, and it can be especially useful at the onset of a cold. The vitamin C in the orange and lime will also help, and the garlic contains powerful antibiotic qualities to prevent infection.

1 large orange, peeled, seeded, and chopped
1 garlic clove
1 lime, peeled, seeded, and chopped
liquid echinacea, as directed on bottle

In a juicer, process the orange, then the garlic and lime. Whisk in the echinacea and serve immediately.
Makes about 3/4 cup (6 fl oz/180 ml); serves 1

Tofu Thick Shake

Soy milk and soy products such as tofu are recommended for women approaching or experiencing menopause, as they contain phytoestrogens that help to balance estrogen levels. When enriched with calcium, they also work to guard against osteoporosis, and may lower blood cholesterol.

1 cup (8 fl oz/250 ml) low-fat, calcium-enriched soy milk
1/4 cup (2 1/2 oz/75 g) silken tofu
1 tablespoon unsweetened cocoa powder
2 teaspoons honey
pinch ground cinnamon

In a blender, combine all the ingredients and blend until smooth and frothy. Serve immediately.
Makes about 1 1/2 cups (12 fl oz/375 ml); serves 1

Right: Berry and Orange Juice

Juice plans

Three-Day Cleansing Juice Plan

There may come a time when you feel that you need an internal "spring cleaning," or would like to change your lifestyle and adopt a healthier diet. A cleansing program is a great way to kick-start a new, healthier way of living. Not only does it help you physically, but it provides a psychological transition between your old and new ways.

The aims of a cleansing program are to reduce the workload of the digestive system, allowing it to perform more efficiently and to also stimulate the parts of the body that are responsible for cleansing and elimination. Probably the most important player is the liver, an organ with many vital functions, including the removal and elimination of toxins in the body. The kidneys also play an important part in removing toxins from the body by filtering them from the blood and eliminating them in the urine.

Some cleansing programs do away with solid food altogether, making a complete fast for the body and allowing just water and perhaps some herbal teas or diluted juices. This is an extreme approach and should not be undertaken without close medical supervision. This plan is not a fast, but a program of light eating that incorporates juices to stimulate the cleansing organs of the body, as well as giving the digestive system a rest.

Besides taking the drinks and eating the foods suggested, a few things must be eliminated during this plan. Avoid coffee, alcohol, cigarettes, and other nonessential drugs. Drink plenty of filtered or spring water, as well as the juices suggested. Avoid salt and oil, and use lemon or lime juice and fresh herbs such as basil, parsley, chives, or cilantro (fresh coriander) to dress and season your food.

Before starting any cleansing program, there are several points to consider.

🌱 If you have any health problems, or are just not sure, tell your doctor or health-care provider what you propose to do and make sure it is okay for your particular requirements.

- ♛ Plan your program to take place over a long weekend, or while you are on holiday, and try to relinquish any responsibilities for those days. Make this time just for you.
- ♛ Be prepared to feel unwell to start with. Cutting out coffee and tea will give you caffeine withdrawal symptoms such as headaches, and you may feel lethargic and hungry due to the change in diet. Persevere; it will be worth it in the end.
- ♛ Don't try to do anything very energetic for the first couple of days. Take gentle walks in the fresh air, read an engrossing novel, or schedule a massage. Create your own health spa at home, but avoid any cosmetic products stronger than a mild massage oil.

Day One

On Rising
2 tablespoons fresh lemon juice in a glass of filtered or spring water

Breakfast
Prune and Apple Drink (page 26)
A small selection of fresh fruit

Mid-morning
Grape and Dandelion Juice (page 26)

Lunch
A salad of raw vegetables, such as red bell pepper (capsicum), celery, lettuce, sprouts, and tomato, sprinkled with fresh herbs and drizzled with lime or lemon juice.

Mid afternoon
Carrot, Apple and Cucumber Juice (page 32)

Dinner
Lightly steamed vegetables such as cauliflower, carrots, onion, and plenty of greens, such as broccoli, spinach, bok choy, and cabbage. Serve with brown rice and season with fresh herbs, fresh lemon juice, and garlic if you like.

Day Two

Repeat the program for Day One, varying the fruits and vegetables if you like, but change the juices to:

Breakfast: Peach, Plum and Raspberry Juice (page 35)

Mid-morning: Beet, Spinach and Pear Juice (page 35)

Mid-afternoon: Wheatgrass Booster (page 90), or Watercress and Orange Juice (page 32)

Day Three

Repeat the program for Day One, changing the juices to:

Breakfast: Super-C Juice (page 94)

Mid-morning: Banana and Mango Frappé (page 39)

Mid-afternoon: Fennel, Pear and Mint Juice (page 30)

The meal suggestions given don't specify quantities; just use your common sense, and even if you feel quite hungry, try not to gorge at mealtimes—your digestive system needs a little R&R. If you feel the need to snack between meals, have a piece of fresh fruit.

Ease back into eating the day after the cleansing program. You may want to have Breakfast in a Glass (page 40), preferably with nondairy milk, or have fresh fruit with some acidophilus yogurt for breakfast.

Add some protein in the form of poached chicken or fish, and vary the starches with potatoes, steamed or baked in their jacket. Fresh fruit and vegetables should be the greater part of your food intake.

Remember, this is the new you, so try not to slip back into the old ways—but don't restrict your diet so much that you feel cheated or resentful. Indulge where socially necessary, and at other times keep yourself nourished and cleansed to cope with the occasional lapse.

Pre-Exam Juice Plan

These drinks contain ingredients with properties that may be useful for anyone who is studying and about to take an exam. It is planned as a "day before" program, but it could be followed at anytime preceding an exam.

Mid-morning: Beet and Carrot Juice with Rosemary (page 47)
Take this juice early in the day to prepare you for effective studying. Rosemary and ginkgo are both said to stimulate the memory, and the carrot and beet are nutrient rich.

Mid-afternoon: Nectarine, Pineapple and Ginseng Drink (page 43)
This is a tasty pick-me-up for when your energy begins to flag. Ginseng increases vitality, helps you to withstand the effects of stress, and will stimulate a tired mind and body.

Before bed: Warm Apple and Chamomile Drink (page 66)
Chamomile helps to reduce anxiety, aid digestion, and is gently sedative, contributing to a good night's sleep.

Extra: Apricot and Bilberry Juice (page 75) may help if your eyes are strained from reading, or if you have been constantly looking at a computer screen.

Tips For Studying

- Good nutrition is needed for an efficient memory, to aid concentration, and generally to keep your mind functioning at its best, in the same way that you need to keep your body nourished to perform physical activity. So always, but especially during a potentially stressful period such as exam time, eat a wide variety of healthy foods.
- Avoid stimulants, such as coffee or soft drinks that contain caffeine, as much as you can. Caffeine may help you to burn the midnight oil, but it will interfere with sleep and ultimately you will end up feeling overtired and unable to unwind.
- Try to organize yourself so that you don't end up having to cram on the day—or worse still—the night before your exam. Research has found that cramming can be counter-productive, with short regular study periods being preferable to one long session the night before.
- Take short breaks while studying. Walk around the room, do some stretches, and take deep breaths. Take care not to use these breaks as opportunities to procrastinate.
- Minimize distractions. Find a place to study where you will not be bombarded with TV noise, music, or conversation.

On the evening before your exam, have a light meal, perhaps a piece of fish with a salad. Do something to take your mind off the next day (and no cramming, remember!), such as renting a funny video or reading an escapist novel. Go to bed early, and rise in time to prepare for the day without having to rush.

Sporting-Event Juice Plan

These suggestions are for drinks and juices to take the day before a sporting event, to fuel you for maximum performance. This plan is not designed for professional athletes, who have specific dietary procedures to follow, according to their sport and training program. Rather, this is intended for, say, a weekend football player who has an important game coming up, or someone taking part in a fun run or an amateur swim meet. These drinks should be incorporated into a varied and nutritious diet.

If you are interested, or planning to become more serious with your sport, contact a sports nutritionist for diet tips and strategies that can enhance your performance.

DAY BEFORE

Breakfast: Fig, Plum and Soy Shake (page 40)
This drink is thick and filling, so you might like to have it for breakfast or as part of the meal along with some whole-grain cereal and fresh fruit. It provides concentrated energy as well as vitamins and minerals to nourish the body.

Late morning: Pear, Peach and Apricot Juice (page 53)
This juice contains fruits with a low glycemic index, so have it around lunch time to help provide sustained energy to get you through an afternoon of training or working out.

Late afternoon: Cantaloupe and Pineapple Recovery Juice (page 54)
Drink this juice when you have finished your exercise for the day. It will help to rehydrate your body and soothe muscle strains that may have occurred.

Eat carbohydrate-rich meals the day before the event. For breakfast, have whole-grain cereal toast and fresh fruit. Lunch will depend on your training schedule, but try to have a filling sandwich or a bowl of soup with some bread, or even a low-fat pasta dish.

At dinner time, have rice, pasta, or potatoes in their jackets as the focus of your meal, with some meat, chicken, or fish for protein and plenty of lightly cooked vegetables, or a salad. Have a hearty meal if you feel like it, particularly if you have been training, but eat a little lighter if you will be going to bed soon after eating.

The Big-Event Juice Plan

The big event could be anything from a wedding, a public performance, or starting a new job—anything that is potentially stressful. As well as taking the suggested drinks to help you through, consider the following strategies.

- ♛ Delegate responsibility and chores where possible. Leave yourself free to focus on the event and your personal preparation.
- ♛ Cut down on stimulants, such as coffee, cola drinks, and cigarettes, as well as alcohol. While these things may give you a little boost and seem to help you through trying times, in the end they will just make you more jittery and debilitated, as well as rob your body of vital nutrients.
- ♛ Eat. When we are stressed or nervous, we tend to get "butterflies" in the stomach, which suppresses the appetite. You may also feel that you do not have time to prepare food and eat it. It is very important to keep the body nourished during times of stress or anxiety, as now more than ever you need to perform and function to the best of your ability.
- ♛ Try to be a day ahead of yourself. When planning a big event such as a wedding, schedule everything that needs to be done one day in advance where possible, giving you the day before the event to relax. This sounds good in theory, although invariably last-minute things will crop up. But it will give you a day to deal with them—and hopefully, a chance to take a little time out.

DAY BEFORE

Morning: Pineapple, Ginger and Lemon Juice (page 69)
This zingy juice gives a good start to the day and provides the digestion-stimulating properties of pineapple and ginger, helping you to cope with food if you are very nervous. Ginger also settles nausea, which can be a side effect of extreme anxiety.

Afternoon: Watermelon Cooler (page 65)
This cooling drink will refresh and soothe an overwrought mind and body, and rehydrate you if you have been neglecting to drink lots of water.

Before bed: Warm Spiced Milk (page 65)
This drink is very nurturing and comforting, and will have you feeling drowsy in no time. Avoid stimulation in the evening, and try to do some relaxation techniques before bed, even if it just telling yourself to "let it all go." Have a light dinner, then a warm bath, drink your milk, and go to bed early.

Glossary

Antihistamines: A substance that eases allergic reactions such as swelling, itching, and redness of the skin.

Anti-inflammatory: A substance that eases inflamed tissue or joints.

Antioxidant: A substance that eliminates free radicals, which are thought to be cancer causing. Vitamins can have antioxidant properties (A, C, and E are the best known), as can minerals, flavonoids, and enzymes.

Anthocyanidin: Flavonoid that forms the blue (or reddish blue) pigment in berries, particularly in bilberries.

Ayurvedic medicine: The traditional wholistic healing system of India.

Beta-carotene: The best known of all carotenoids, which is converted to vitamin A in the body. It is particularly rich in carrots.

Bioflavonoids or flavonoids: The colorful pigments in some fruits and vegetables, which is also present in citrus pith and membrane. They have antioxidant properties, as well as other health applications.

Carotenoids: Plant pigments that give fruits and vegetables a red, orange, or yellow color.

Diuretic: A substance that increases the excretion of urine.

Enzymes: Proteins that act as a catalyst for metabolic functions in the body, such as breaking down foods so the body can absorb the nutrients.

Expectorant: A substance that causes mucus in the respiratory system to loosen and be expelled.

Free radicals: Incomplete oxygen molecules that attack and oxidize other molecules. Antioxidants work to allay this reaction. The body can tolerate a certain amount of free-radical activity, but when it exceeds the capacity of antioxidants present, cell damage can occur.

Fructose: The natural sugar present in fruit, which gives it a sweet flavor.

Glycemic index: A measure of the rate at which carbohydrate foods cause blood sugar levels to rise.

Laxative: A substance that stimulates excretion from the bowel.

Osteoporosis: A condition where the bones become very brittle and vulnerable to breaks and fractures. It occurs most commonly, though not exclusively, in late-middle-aged and elderly women.

Phytoestrogens: Estrogens found in plants, which are similar to the female hormone estrogen.

Ingredients Index

Health Index

Guide to Weights and Measures

WEIGHTS

Imperial	Metric
$1/3$ oz	10 g
$1/2$ oz	15 g
$3/4$ oz	20 g
1 oz	30 g
2 oz	60 g
3 oz	90 g
4 oz ($1/4$ lb)	125 g
5 oz ($1/3$ lb)	150 g
6 oz	180 g
7 oz	220 g
8 oz ($1/2$ lb)	250 g
9 oz	280 g
10 oz	300 g
11 oz	330 g
12 oz ($3/4$ lb)	375 g
16 oz (1 lb)	500 g
2 lb	1 kg
3 lb	1.5 kg
4 lb	2 kg

VOLUME

Imperial	Metric	Cup
1 fl oz	30 ml	
2 fl oz	60 ml	$1/4$
3	90 ml	$1/3$
4	125 ml	$1/2$
5	150 ml	$2/3$
6	180 ml	$3/4$
8	250 ml	1
10	300 ml	$1^1/4$
12	375 ml	$1^1/2$
13	400 ml	$1^2/3$
14	440 ml	$1^3/4$
16	500 ml	2
24	750 ml	3
32	1L	4

USEFUL CONVERSIONS

$1/4$ teaspoon	1.25 ml
$1/2$ teaspoon	2.5 ml
1 teaspoon	5 ml
1 Australian tablespoon	20 ml (4 teaspoons)
1 UK/US tablespoon	15 ml (3 teaspoons)

Butter/Shortening

1 tablespoon	$1/2$ oz	15 g
$1^1/2$ tablespoons	$3/4$ oz	20 g
2 tablespoons	1 oz	30 g
3 tablespoons	$1^1/2$ oz	45 g

OVEN TEMPERATURE GUIDE

The Celsius (°C) and Fahrenheit (°F) temperatures in this chart apply to most electric ovens. Decrease by 25°F or 10°C for a gas oven or refer to the manufacturer's temperature guide. For temperatures below 325°F (160°C), do not decrease the given temperature.

Oven description	°C	°F	Gas Mark
Cool	110	225	$1/4$
	130	250	$1/2$
Very slow	140	275	1
	150	300	2
Slow	170	325	3
Moderate	180	350	4
	190	375	5
Moderately Hot	200	400	6
Fairly Hot	220	425	7
Hot	230	450	8
Very Hot	240	475	9
Extremely Hot	250	500	10

First published in the United States in 2002 by Periplus Editions (HK) Ltd.,
with editorial offices at 153 Milk Street, Boston, Massachusetts 02109 and
130 Joo Seng Road #06-01/03
Olivine Building, Singapore 368357

© Copyright 2002 Lansdowne Publishing Pty Ltd

Commissioned by Deborah Nixon
Text: Tracy Rutherford
Photographer: Scott Hawkins
Stylist: Suzie Smith
Designer: Robyn Latimer
Editor: Carolyn Miller
Production Manager: Sally Stokes
Project Coordinator: Alexandra Nahlous

All rights reserved. No part of this publication may be reproduced or utilized in any form or by any means,
electronic or mechanical, including photocopying, recording, or by any information storage and
retrieval system, without prior written permission from the publisher.

Library of Congress Cataloging-in-Publication Data is available.
ISBN 0-7946-5011-2

DISCLAIMER
This book is intended to give general information only and is not a substitute for professional and medical advice.
Consult your health care provider before adopting any of the treatments contained in this book. The publisher,
author and distributor expressly disclaim all liability to any person arising directly or indirectly from the use of,
or for any errors or omissions in, the information in this book. The adoption and application of the information
in this book is at the reader's discretion and is his or her sole responsibility.

DISTRIBUTED BY

North America	Japan and Korea	Asia Pacific
Tuttle Publishing	Tuttle Publishing	Berkeley Books Pte. Ltd.
Distribution Center	RK Building, 2nd Floor	130 Joo Seng Road
Airport Industrial Park	2-13-10 Shimo-Meguro,	#06-01/03
364 Innovation Drive	Meguro-Ku	Olivine Building
North Clarendon, VT 05759-9436	Tokyo 153 0064	Singapore 368357
Tel: (802) 773-8930	Tel: (03) 5437-0171	Tel: (65) 280-3320
Tel: (800) 526-2778	Fax: (03) 5437-0755	Fax: (65) 280-6290
Fax: (802) 773-6993		

Set in Giovanni Book on QuarkXPress
Printed in Singapore

First Edition
07 06 05 04 03 02   10 9 8 7 6 5 4 3 2 1